Getting Skills Right

Community Education and Training in South Africa

OECD
BETTER POLICIES FOR BETTER LIVES

Please cite this publication as:
OECD (2019), *Community Education and Training in South Africa*, Getting Skills Right, OECD Publishing, Paris.
https://doi.org/10.1787/9789264312302-en

ISBN 978-92-64-31229-6 (print)
ISBN 978-92-64-31230-2 (pdf)

Getting Skills Right
ISSN 2520-6117 (print)
ISSN 2520-6125 (online)

Photo credits: Cover © Cell phone: © Creative Commons/Alfredo Hernandez, clock: © Creative Commons/Hakan Yalcin, cloud upload: Creative Commons/Warslab, join: © Creative Commons/Tom Ingebretsen, doctor: © Creative Commons/Joseph Wilson, chef: © Creative Commons/Alfonso Melolontha.

Corrigenda to OECD publications may be found on line at: *www.oecd.org/about/publishing/corrigenda.htm*.

Foreword

Under the impulse of global megatrends, such as technological progress and globalisation, the demand for and supply of skills has undergone substantial changes in recent decades. These changes can result in skills imbalances which can have strongly negative consequences for individuals, firms and societies. Individuals whose skills are not in demand in the labour market could face prolonged periods of joblessness, increasing the risk of poverty. When skills imbalances in the labour market are big, firms can have persistent difficulties in finding the right people, which could negatively affect their productivity. For societies as a whole, these imbalances could have a negative impact on growth and the overall well-being of the country.

Skills imbalances can be tackled through a range of policy interventions, including education and training, employment and migration policies. One of the key policy areas that can contribute to lower skills imbalances is lifelong learning. Adults who have left initial education, should invest regularly in keeping their skills up-to-date with what is needed in the labour market.

This report takes a closer look at lifelong learning in South Africa, with a focus on education and training activities provided by the Community Education and Training system. The report is structured as follows. Section 1 presents key statistics to show the urgency for investment in lifelong learning in South Africa. In Section 2 the current state of the Community Education and Training system in South Africa is described. Section 3 analyses the role that Community Education and Training could play, while Section 4 looks at possible funding mechanisms. Section 5 explores the topic of aligning training provision in the Community Education and Training system with local labour market and community needs, and Section 6 discusses the quality assurance of the system.

This work fits into a broader programme of work of the OECD on the functioning, effectiveness and resilience of adult learning systems across countries, and builds on the extensive work of the OECD in the area of skills, including rich analyses on the alignment between skills demand and supply, vocational education and training, and work-based learning.

The work on this report was carried out by Marieke Vandeweyer from the Skills and Employability Division of the Directorate for Employment, Labour and Social Affairs, with contributions by Pauline Musset from the OECD Centre for Skills. The work was supervised by Glenda Quintini (team manager on skills) and Mark Keese (Head of the Skills and Employability Division). The report has benefited from helpful comments provided by the Department for Higher Education and Training, and participants to a dedicated workshop organised in Johannesburg in October 2018.

This report is published under the responsibility of the Secretary-General of the OECD, with the financial assistance of the JPMorgan Chase Foundation. The views expressed in this report should not be taken to reflect the official position of the JPMorgan Chase Foundation.

Acronyms and abbreviations

A(B)ET	Adult (Basic) Education and Training
B-BBEE	Broad-based black economic empowerment
CET	Community Education and Training
CLC	Community Learning Centre
CWP	Community Works Programme
DBE	Department of Basic Education
DHET	Department of Higher Education and Training
DoL	Department of Labour
EPWP	Expanded Public Works Programme
ESSA	Employment Services South Africa
GDP	Gross Domestic Product
GETCA	General Education and Training Certificate for Adults
HEI	Higher Education Institution
NASCA	National Senior Certificate for Adults
NCV	National Certificate Vocational
NGO	Non-Governmental Organisation
NQF	National Qualifications Framework
NSC	National Senior Certificate
NSF	National Skills Fund
OECD	Organisation for Economic Co-operation and Development
PALC	Public Adult Learning Centre
PES	Public Employment Service
RPL	Recognition of Prior Learning
SAQA	South African Qualifications Authority
SETA	Sector Education and Training Authority
SME	Small and Medium-sized Enterprise
TVET	Technical and Vocational Education and Training
UIF	Unemployment Insurance Fund

Table of contents

Tables

Figures

Boxes

Follow OECD Publications on:

http://twitter.com/OECD_Pubs

http://www.facebook.com/OECDPublications

http://www.linkedin.com/groups/OECD-Publications-4645871

http://www.youtube.com/oecdilibrary

OECD Alerts

http://www.oecd.org/oecddirect/

Executive summary

Unemployment in South Africa remains persistently high, especially for low-skilled youth and adults. Upper secondary education (i.e. the National Senior Certificate) has become a minimum requirement for many jobs, and employers are looking for workers with strong cognitive and technical skills. While educational attainment is on the rise in South Africa, many students still leave initial education without an upper secondary degree. Today, around 19 million South African adults, or 57% of the South African adult population, do not have an upper secondary degree. At the same time, opportunities for adults to participate in training after leaving initial education are scarce. There is a strong need for more and better second chance education and training opportunities for adults who are in need of up-skilling or re-skilling to gain sustained access to jobs.

The notion of Community Education and Training has been around in South Africa for many years, but was made more concrete in the 2013 White Paper for Post-school Education and Training. According to the White Paper, the role of Community Education and Training is to facilitate a cycle of lifelong learning in communities by enabling the development of skills (including literacy, numeracy and vocational skills) to enhance personal, social, family and employment experiences. The ambitious target of one million students in Community Education and Training institutions by 2030, compared to the 273 000 adults enrolled today, highlighted the commitment of the government to make this new training system work. Nonetheless, the current Community Education and Training system remains underdeveloped. The system was kick started by taking over the previous adult (basic) education system that provided second chance secondary education. Not much progress has been made in practice since to expand or improve the system, and limited public funding has been channelled towards it. The system remains plagued by high dropout rates, low quality, limited visibility and poor image. Reaching the target of 1 million students will be hard, and it should be ensured that there is no trade-off between quantity and quality.

The goal of this report is to propose concrete action that could be taken to get the Community Education and Training system going. The report focuses on four topics: i) the role of Community Education and Training, ii) how to finance the system, iii) the alignment of training with community needs, and iv) quality assurance. Throughout the report, international good practice examples are provided to point to potential solutions for the challenges encountered. The key insights from the different chapters are:

- For Community Education and Training to respond to community needs, it should not only provide academic second chance opportunities and remedial literacy and numeracy programmes, but also vocational skills programmes and non-formal programmes, such as employability, entrepreneurship and life-skills training. Additionally, the delivery sites of Community Education and Training should be places where youth and adults can obtain information about further education and training and labour market opportunities, and where recognition of prior learning can take place.

- It is unlikely in the short-run that substantial additional central government funding can be mobilised for Community Education and Training, especially in light of the substantial additional funding that has recently been committed to higher education. The funds collected form employers through the skills development levy must be used more effectively, and the National Skills Fund needs to focus more on training opportunities for disadvantaged groups. There needs to be better coordination with other stakeholders that are funding training opportunities (e.g. the provincial and municipal government, the unemployment insurance fund), and these opportunities need to be better promoted and made accessible for low-skilled adults.
- The Community Education and Training system needs to cooperate closely with local stakeholders from the community, to ensure that the training programmes and services provided in delivery sites respond to real community needs. The delivery sites should have sufficient flexibility to adapt the training offer and content to the needs and realities in their communities. Strong engagement with local community members will also facilitate cooperation in terms of facility sharing and job placements of graduates.
- Improving the quality of training opportunities at Community Education and Training institutions is crucial if they are to contribute significantly to better livelihoods of participants. Quality should be enhanced by ensuring that teachers have the relevant skills to deliver a diversified set of programmes to adult learners and that management and support staff have the capabilities to fulfil their new and broader roles. Putting in place adequate and transparent quality assurance mechanisms will also be crucial for ensuring high quality provision.

One key message that emerges throughout the report is the need for strong coordination and cooperation between the Community Education and Training system and other relevant stakeholders. Many actors are currently providing or financing training activities of job-seekers and workers, and rather than duplicating what they are already doing, the Community Education and Training system should bring those actors together and better inform youth and adults about existing training opportunities. The Community Education and Training system does not need to re-invent the wheel, rather it should bring transparency into the existing training offer, fill the gaps in this training offer and facilitate access to training for low-skilled adults.

The action steps proposed in this report focus on the short to medium run, keeping in mind the tight budgetary situation of the Community Education and Training system. Much more ambitious actions should be envisaged for the long-run, especially in view of reaching the targets from the White Paper. In addition, improvements to other parts of the education and training system are imperative, particularly in basic education and technical and vocational education and training. It should also be noted that the high unemployment rate in South Africa is not only driven by supply-side factors, and policies to stimulate the demand for labour and improve job quality are crucial to improve employment prospects of the South African population.

Assessment and recommendations

The Community Education and Training system has the potential to fill an important gap in training provision in South Africa, especially for low-skilled job seekers and workers. Various actors, both private and public, already provide training opportunities, but provision is scattered and many adults in need of up-skilling or re-skilling do not participate in training. Increasing access to training can help tackling existing skills imbalances and contribute to lower unemployment, poverty and inequality.

Currently, Community Education and Training institutions mainly provide second chance primary and secondary education. However, to make the system more useful and accessible for adults, a wider range of programmes and services should be provided, in line with local needs. While second chance education should remain an important component of Community Education and Training, the offer should be extended to vocational and non-formal education and training programmes, as well as information and guidance services. At the same time, existing and new programmes need to be adapted to the specific needs of adult learners.

In order to provide a wider range of programmes and services, and to reach the objective of one million students in Community Education and Training by 2030, substantial investments is needed. Only a very small part of the public budget is currently allocated to the Community Education and Training system, and substantial increases are unlikely in the present economic climate and in view of the significant resources needed to support fee-free access to higher education for lower-income students. To secure sufficient funding for the further development of the Community Education and Training system, alternative sources need to be mobilised. The National Skills Fund should re-focus on training opportunities for vulnerable groups, and SETAs should spend the skills development levy funds more effectively. Stronger coordination with other stakeholders funding training, including provincial and municipal governments and the Unemployment Insurance Fund, are key in reaching the common goal of higher access to training.

For Community Education and Training to have a real impact, it should be responsive to the needs of the community. Institutions need to have sufficient flexibility to adapt the training offer and content to these needs. Strong coordination with local stakeholders is crucial to identify community needs, but also to develop partnerships with employers and other education and training providers. Staff in Community Education and Training institutions need to have easy access to existing information on community needs and need to develop the knowledge and skills to actively engage with stakeholders.

Finally, the potential impact of an expanded Community Education and Training system crucially depends on the quality of programmes and services provided. Quality assurance in the current system is very scattered because of the variety of programmes offered, and a more transparent system should be put in place to ensure that all training programmes comply with a minimum standard. At the same time, further investment in the skills of teachers, school leaders and support staff need to be made to ensure that they can carry out their tasks effectively.

Box 1. Key recommendations for Community Education and Training

Providing a diverse set of training programmes and services

Basic skills programmes and second chance lower and upper secondary education

- Design a basic skills programme to be delivered in Community Education and Training (CET) institutions, building on insights and materials from the Kha Ri Gude campaign.
- Develop learning materials for second chance lower and upper secondary education that provide an integrated approach to basic adult education.
- Support the progress of students from basic skills programmes into second chance secondary education.

Vocational skills programmes

- Take stock of the already available vocational skills training programmes in the local communities, and decide on which training programmes to offer at CET institutions and which external providers to enter into partnerships with.
- Engage with local employers and Sector Education and Training Authorities (SETAs) to make sure that internship opportunities are available for CET students.
- Coordinate closely with Technical and Vocational Education and Training (TVET) colleges in the region to ensure that there are easy pathways from the CET vocational skills programmes into TVET programmes.

Non-formal programmes

- Decide on which non-formal programmes to offer and their content in close cooperation with local NGOs, employers and government departments.
- Develop standardized CET certificates that serve as proof of (successful) completion of some of the non-formal programmes.

Information, guidance and recognition of prior learning (RPL)

- Train CET staff to be able to deliver guidance in terms of training and job opportunities. Counsellors should keep their knowledge up-to-date through regular training.
- Develop materials that can be used by CET staff to assist individuals in the elaboration of their RPL portfolio, and organise information sessions on RPL.
- Facilitate coordination between CET institutions and Labour Centres, so that they can exchange information on job and training opportunities.

Ensuring adequate investment and securing the necessary funding

Priority investment areas

- Audit the availability of empty spaces in communities where CET institutions now operate in poor conditions, and make agreements with other training providers to use their facilities.
- Review the staffing in CET institutions and hire additional staff where needed. Develop training courses to get current staff members ready for their new tasks and roles.
- Develop teaching and learning materials that allow for flexible and modular approaches. Coordinate with TVET colleges, employers, NGOs and government departments to obtain the necessary teaching and learning materials for vocational and non-formal programmes.
- Take stock of available IT resources in the communities that could be used in CET institutions or be made accessible to CET students (e.g. libraries, enterprises).

Potential funding sources

- Coordinate with provincial and municipal governments to understand the training programmes they fund/offer, and ensure that they see CET as a potential partner.
- Submit a concrete and realistic funding request with the Treasury. A positive answer is more likely when the request concerns concrete plans that have political support.
- Re-focus the National Skills Fund so that it is better targeted at the unemployed and other disadvantaged groups, and earmark a substantial part of its budget for CET investment.

- Set more ambitious targets for SETAs in terms of training, especially in light of the growing levy collection and consistent underspending. Make all basic skills, second change, vocational and non-formal job-related programmes in CET eligible for SETA funding.
- Allocate a larger part of the Unemployment Insurance Fund surplus to training expenditure as a way to improve labour market entry of job-seekers.

Aligning provision with local needs

Flexibility in programme offering and content

- Design curricula for the centrally determined training programmes, in consultation with key stakeholders. Develop general teaching and learning materials for non-formal programmes.
- Train CET managers on understanding the unit standards system and on curriculum design. This should be done in cooperation with SETAs and TVET colleges.

Using available skill needs information

- Set up information sessions for CET staff to get familiar with existing skill needs data. Create a digital platform where all skill needs information is brought together.
- Coordinate with SETAs and Employment Services South Africa to obtain skills needs information at the local level.

Involving key local stakeholders

- Train CET managers on how to engage with local stakeholders.
- Invite identified key stakeholders for information sessions on their potential role in CET. Engage with stakeholders on a regular basis, to ensure that the course offering and content remains in line with local needs.
- Set up an information system to document stakeholder engagement. The evaluation of CET institutions should take their performance in stakeholder engagement into account.

Taking outcomes and feedback into account

- Administer standardised satisfaction surveys and set up an information system to bring together the survey results.
- Carefully register all students, including contact details. This could (in the future) be used for tracing surveys or for linking the CET database to other databases.

Ensuring high quality provision

Improving the quality of the CET workforce

- Make sure that lecturers in the CET system are qualified, by gradually implementing training policies using professional development and RPL mechanisms.
- Develop flexible pathways into the teaching profession for vocational subjects. Facilitate the entry of skilled workers from industry through shortened pedagogical preparation.

Developing a quality framework

- Map out existing quality assurance and accreditation systems and improve their transparency
- Develop, in consultation with stakeholders, quality standards and self-evaluation tools for CET institutions to measure performance against these standards.
- Develop an accreditation system based on the quality standards, to ensure that all institutions are of quality and meet minimum requirements.
- Develop a monitoring system for institutions to help them improve and collect data about learners, lecturers and institutions, including on learners' socio-economic background.

Chapter 1. The urgency of lifelong learning in South Africa

This chapter provides some key background information on the South African labour market, as well as the skills and education outcomes of adults. It focusses specifically on participation in post-school education and training and training opportunities provided by employers. This information contributes to a better understanding of the training needs among South African adults, and the role that a community education and training system could potentially play.

1.1. Many South Africans do not have access to the labour market

In recent decades, the South African labour market has experienced persistently high unemployment rates (Figure 1.1). In the final quarter of 2018, 6.139 million South Africans were unemployed, representing 27.1% of the labour force. A further 2.841 million people were willing to work but not actively looking for a job (i.e. discouraged job seekers). With an unemployment rate fluctuating around 50% during the last years, the labour market situation for youth in South Africa is particularly problematic. When adding the discouraged job seekers to the group of unemployed, the youth unemployment rate rises to 66%. Labour market outcomes differ strongly between population groups, with the black African population having an unemployment rate that is almost 4.5 times as high as the unemployment rate of the White population. In addition, differences between provinces are substantial (StatsSA, 2019[1]). Poor and unequal labour market opportunities have contributed to high poverty rates and a level of income inequality that is much higher than in OECD countries.

Figure 1.1. The unemployment rate in South Africa is high, especially for youth

Unemployment rate (%)

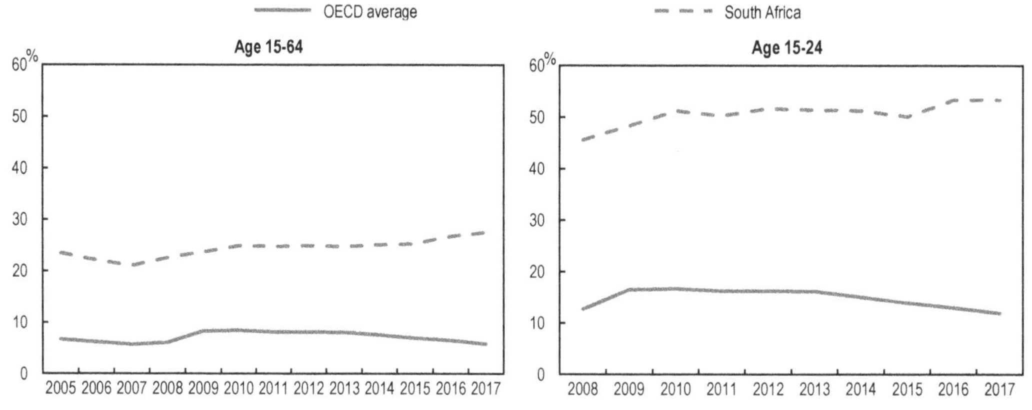

Source: OECD Short-term labour market statistics database.

Investment in skills has a clear positive impact on labour market outcomes in South Africa. The unemployment rate of individuals who completed upper-secondary education (i.e. Matric holders) is 4 percentage points lower than that of individuals without a Matric degree, who have an unemployment rate as high as 32% (in the final quarter of 2017). However, the biggest impact on unemployment comes from obtaining a higher education degree: Only 6.7% of adults with a higher education degree were unemployed in the final quarter of 2018, compared to 28% of matric holders. Graduating from a TVET college also reduces the probability of being unemployed (to 16%), albeit to a lesser extent than for university graduates.[1] (StatsSA, 2019[1])

1.2. Educational attainment is on the rise, but dropout remains high

Despite the large benefits of educational investment, many South Africans have low education levels. According to Aitchison (2016[2]), South Africa counts around 5 million people who are functionally illiterate. Educational attainment statistics show that over 19 million adults, i.e. 57% of the South African adult population, do not have an upper secondary degree (i.e. a National Senior Certificate or Matric degree).[2] However, more and more South Africans are obtaining their Matric degree: among the population aged 25-34 there are only 51% that did not obtain the Matric degree (Figure 1.2). While the higher completion rates of upper secondary education are a positive evolution, progress remains slow in comparison to OECD countries and other emerging economies like Brazil, India and Indonesia.[3] Progression in terms of lower secondary education completion has been much faster: only 12.1% of youth (18-25 years old) did not finish Grade 9, while this is 21.8% among all adults (aged 18 to 64).[4]

Figure 1.2. Many South Africans do not have an upper secondary degree

Educational attainment of the adult population (2015)

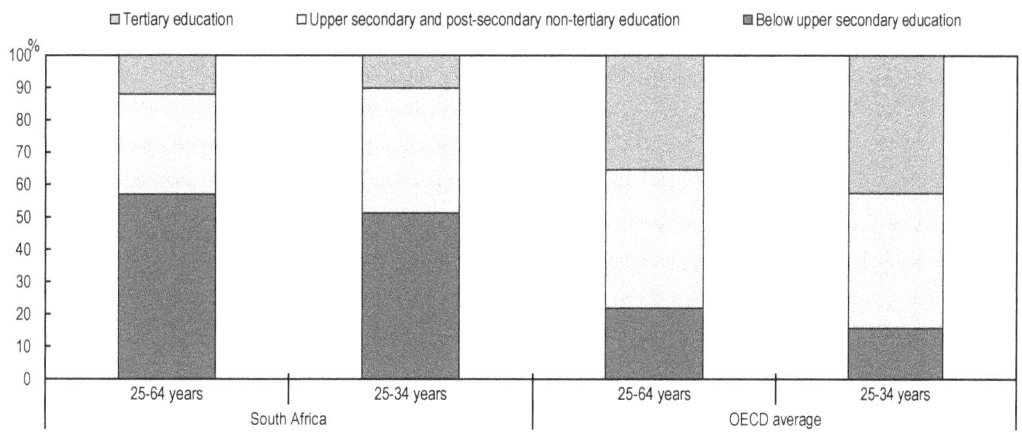

Note: Data for the OECD average refer to the latest available year. Upper secondary in South Africa refers to completed Grade 12/NSC.
Source: OECD ($2017_{[3]}$).

While there is almost universal enrolment in the compulsory education phase (Grade 1 to 9) in South Africa, dropout rates are substantial after Grade 9. Many students do not reach Grade 12. Estimates from Simkins ($2013_{[4]}$) show that only around 70% of students who do not progress into TVET education after Grade 9 make it to Grade 12.

Even for those who finish Grade 12 further options are often limited and they find themselves at a dead-end. In 2017, 75.1% of students who enrolled for the Matric exam obtained the pass mark, among which three out of four were eligible to register for studies at higher education institutions. A recent analysis of the 2008 matric cohort showed that 31.5% of students with a bachelor pass did not enrol in undergraduate studies in the years following their matric graduation, and that among those who did enrol 30% dropped out (Van Broekhuizen, Van Der Berg and Hofmeyr, $2017_{[5]}$). The combination of high dropout rates and low pass-through to university imply that only 4% of school starters eventually obtain a university degree (within six years of obtaining their Matric degree).

Education quality is an issue too in South Africa. International student assessment exercises show that South African students in basic education perform poorly in mathematics and science. According to the results from the 2015 Trends in International Mathematics and Science Study (TIMSS) assessment, South African Grade 4 learners ranked 48th out of 49 countries in mathematics, while Grade 8 learners ranked 38th out of 39 in mathematics and last in science.[5] The 2016 Progress in International Reading Literacy Study (PIRLS) results show that South African Grade 4 students have lower reading abilities than students in any of the 50 participating countries. Similarly, South African Grade 6 students scored below the cross-country average in mathematics and reading in the 2000 and 2007 tests of the Southern and Eastern Africa Consortium for Monitoring Educational Quality (SACMEQ), which assess student skills in Southern and Eastern African countries. Looking at the evolution of skill levels over time, the 2012 and 2015 waves of the TIMSS assessment show a significant improvement in student skills compared to previous years, but South Africa's performance remains low compared to countries at a similar stage of development (Reddy et al., 2015[6]; Gustafsson, 2017[7]).

1.3. Few adults participate in training activities after leaving initial education

After leaving initial education, adults can participate in a range of lifelong learning activities to improve their skills further. In South Africa, adults who want to obtain high-school equivalent training can enrol in Adult Education and Training (AET) centres, which have recently been rebranded as Community Education and Training Centres (see Chapter 2). In 2016 around 27 000 adults were enrolled in 2 778 centres, 8% less than in 2011 (Figure 1.3). The most popular AET programme is Level 4 training (i.e. equivalent to Grade 9), followed by Grade 12 training. Information about the characteristics of adults participating in these programmes is very scant, but according to evidence from a sample of AET centres shows that the majority of participants are between 19 and 24 years old (Lolwana, Rabe and Morakane, 2018[8]).

Figure 1.3. Adults have access to a range of training programmes

Number of registered participants

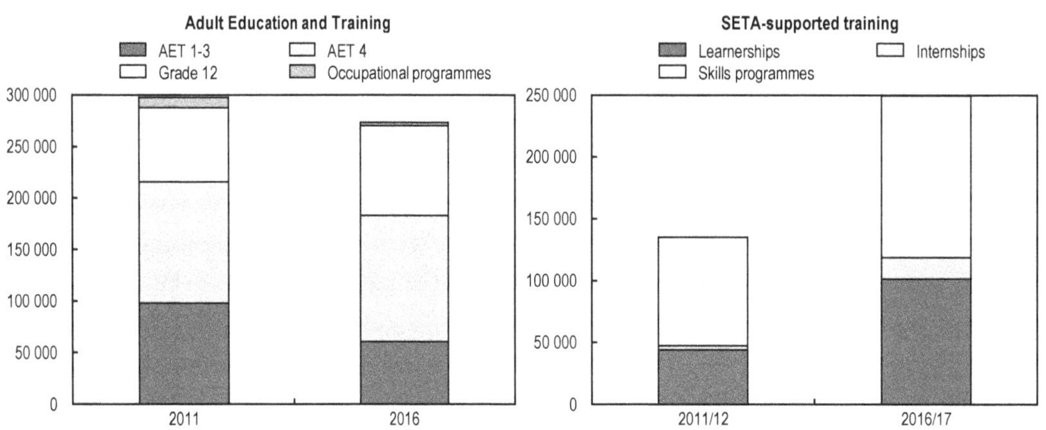

Note: Grade 12 also includes participants in Grade 10 and 11, but the numbers are insignificant (478 in 2011 and 1633 in 2016).
Source: Department for Higher Education and Training (2016[9])

Participation of adults in lifelong learning often takes the form of job-related training to develop or enhance job- or occupation-specific skills. The only data available on participation in this type of training activities in South Africa relates to training supported by Sector Education and Training Authorities (SETA), which includes learnerships, internships and skills programmes. SETAs play an important role in skills development in South Africa (see Box 1.1 for details on the role of SETAs). In 2016/17, 250 000 adults participated in SETA-supported training programmes, of which over half were unemployed. Participation in SETA-supported training increased by 85% in the period

2011/12 to 2016/17 (Figure 1.3). Nonetheless, the total number of participants represents only a very small share of the total labour force (around 1.1%), suggesting that access to this type of training is low. However, employers could be providing training outside of the SETA-support system, and the World Bank Enterprise Survey suggests that in 2007 37% of South African employers were providing training.[6] The main public incentives for South African employers to provide training are described in Box 1.2.

Box 1.1. Sector Education and Training Authorities in South Africa

Following the 1998 Skills Development Act, 23 SETAs were created in 2000, each with their own clearly defined sectors. The members of SETAs represent organised labour and employers, and relevant government departments. After the responsibility for SETAs was transferred from the Department of Labour to the Department for Higher Education and Training, the number of SETAs was reduced to 21 in 2011.

According to the (amended) Skills Development Act, the main functions of SETAs include:

- Analysing skill needs in the sectors through Sector Skills Plans
- Implementing the Sector Skills Plan by establishing learning programmes, approving employers' workplace skills plans and annual training reports, allocating grants to employers, education and training providers and workers, monitoring education and training
- Promoting learning programmes (including identifying workplaces for practical work experience and supporting the development of learning) and registering agreements for learning programmes
- Collecting and disbursing the skills development levy
- Liaising with the National Skills Authority, the public employment service, education bodies, provincial skills development forums, and the Quality Council for Trades and Occupations

Lifelong learning for adults can also take the form of participation in formal education at the post-secondary and tertiary level. Unfortunately, available enrolment data in TVET and higher education institutions does not allow distinguishing between students who continue straight from lower- or upper-secondary education and adults who had already left initial education and entered the labour market. To complicate measurement further, some of the participants in SETA supported training from Figure 1.3 will be taking their training in TVET or higher education institutions. In 2016, 1.143 million students were enrolled in higher education institutions, i.e. 16% more than in 2010 (Figure 1.4). The number of students in public TVET colleges almost doubled during the same period, reaching 705 000 in 2016.[7] Seven out of ten TVET students are enrolled in N1-N6 (Nated) programmes (see details on the different vocational programmes in Chapter 3), the majority of whom at the post-secondary level (N4-N6).

Figure 1.4 shows that both TVET and higher education institutions are mainly attended by youth: 70% of TVET students and 55% of university students are younger than 25, while 26% and 28%, respectively, are aged 25-34 (Department of Higher Education and Training, 2016[9]).[8] These data, however, also suggest that many students do not directly advance from secondary education into TVET or higher education, but first spend some time in the labour market or in inactivity. The age profile of students also shows that not many TVET students are younger than 20 years old. This suggests that TVET does not provide an alternative to the academic route (i.e. the grade 10-12 route towards Matric) after Grade 9. Field, Musset and Álvarez-Galván (2014[10]) already noted that too many Matric graduates wanting to enter vocational programmes at the post-school level were expected to start at the vocational training upper-secondary level.

Box 1.2. Incentives for South African employers to provide training opportunities

Skills Development Levy

All firms in South Africa with a wage bill of at least ZAR 500 000 pay a levy equal to 1% of their total annual wage bill. The collected levies are distributed to the National Skills Fund (NSF) (20%) and the SETAs (80%). SETAs redistribute the funds to employers under the form of mandatory and discretionary grants. Employers who submit their annual training report and workplace skills plan receive the mandatory grant, equal to 20% of the levy. Discretionary grants are given to employers for specific training requests, and are only available for employers who are eligible for the mandatory grants (i.e. employers who submitted the required documents). Since 2012, 80% of the discretionary grants is earmarked for formal training in scarce and critical skills, as identified by the SETAs. In 2015/16 the SETAs received just over ZAR 12 billion through the levy system. Generally, SETAs have not been spending all their funds, and have therefore been accumulating reserves.

Broad-based black economic empowerment (B-BBEE)

Firms in South Africa have to comply with B-BBEE, based on a B-BBEE scorecard. The objective of B-BBEE is to transform the economy and enhance the economic participation of the black African population. The B-BBEE score of firms is based on i) equity ownership, ii) management control, iii) skills development, iv) enterprise development, and v) socio-economic development. The benefit of having a high B-BBEE score is that government entities have to consider B-BBEE scores when using services of private sector firms. Private sector firms may also adopt their own B-BBEE requirements when working with other firms. In the area of skills development, firms need to spend 6% of their total annual wage bill on training of black African workers or job seekers to get the highest B-BBEE score. Additional points are awarded for learnerships and internships, training of unemployed individuals, and the absorption of unemployed learners at the end of the learnership programme.

Learnership tax incentive

A learnership tax incentive was introduced in 2006, giving employers a tax refund on commencement of a learnership, and a second one on completion. The tax incentive was renewed for five more years in 2016. Since 2016, higher tax credits apply for learnerships on levels 1 to 6 of the National Qualifications Framework (NQF), targeting the incentive more towards technical skills development.

Source: OECD (2017[11]); B-BBEE Commission (2016[12]); DNA Economics (2016[13])

Figure 1.4. The number of students in public TVET institutions is growing steadily

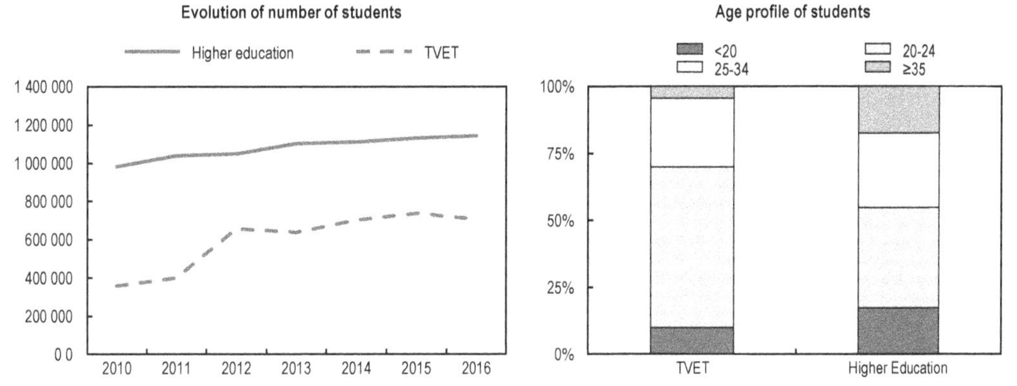

Note: The data for the age profile of students refers to 2016 for TVET students and 2013 for higher education students. The age groups in the higher education data are <20, 20-24, 25-35 and >35, and only refer to students from public institutions.
Source: Department for Higher Education and Training (2016[9]), Council on Higher Education (2016[14]).

1.4. Government funding priorities lie with higher education

Government expenditure on post-school education and training increased steadily over the last few years, and this trend is expected to continue in the medium-term (Table 1.1). In the financial year 2017/2018, expenditure on universities accounted for 81% of total expenditure, and TVET for 14.4%. Only ZAR 2.198 billion, or 4.2% of total expenditure, was allocated to Community Education and Training (i.e. the former AET system). Because of the decision to provide free higher and TVET education to students from low-income households, expenditure on university and TVET education is expected to increase drastically in the next few years. Expenditure on higher education and TVET is planned to almost double in the period 2017/18 to 2020/21. The budget allocated to Community Education and Training will also see an increase (+23.5%), reflecting the government's plan to significantly expand the opportunities for adults without a degree to participate in education and training, but its share will remain very small in the overall budget (2.8%). Expenditure on skills development represents an insignificant part of the budget, which reflects the fact that skills development programmes are mainly financed by SETAs and the National Skills Fund (NSF) (and hence not included in the government budget numbers). According to the National Treasury (2018[15]), the number of workers and unemployed completing a SETA-sponsored skills programme or learnership is expected to increase by 21% in the period 2016/17 to 2020/21, while the number of persons benefiting from NSF funding is expected to increase by 61% in the same period[9].

To put these numbers in perspective, the 2017/18 expenditure on basic education amounts to ZAR 231.6 billion, which is equivalent to 16.5% of total government expenditure. Total government expenditure on post-school education and training only accounts for 6.8% of total expenditure. In contrast, the projected medium-term growth rate of expenditure on post-school education and training is the largest among all budget items, largely exceeding growth of basic education expenditure. (National Treasury, 2018[15])

Table 1.1. National government expenditure on post-school education and training is on the rise

Audited and estimated expenditure (in million ZAR)

	Audited expenditure		Medium-term expenditure estimate	Growth (2017/18-2020/21)
	2013/14	2017/18	2020/21	
University education	28 303. 3	41 931.7	80 666.2	92.4%
TVET	5 879.3	7 460.2	14 585.1	95.5%
Community Education and Training	1 776.8	2 197.7	2 714.7	23.5%
Skills Development	123.0	249.4	297.0	19.1%
Total	36 082.4	51 830.9	98 263	89.6%

Note: The budget for higher education and training also includes the categories Administration and Planning, Policy and Strategy, which are not included in this table. In the financial year 2017/18 these two categories accounted jointly for ZAR 468.7 million or 0.9% of the total budget.
Source: National Treasury (2017[16]; 2018[15])

1.5. Skills imbalances need to be addressed

The combination of low educational attainment, poor education quality and limited participation in lifelong learning activities increases the probability of substantial skills imbalances. As documented by OECD (2017[11]; 2017[17]), South Africa faces shortages of skills in certain areas and many South Africans work in jobs that do not match their level or field of qualification. Shortages are mainly found for cognitive skills and abilities, such as verbal abilities, reasoning abilities and complex problem-solving skills, and for knowledge in the field of education and training (Figure 1.5).

Figure 1.5. High-level cognitive skills are in shortage

Degree of shortage (+) and surplus (-) of abilities, skills and knowledge types

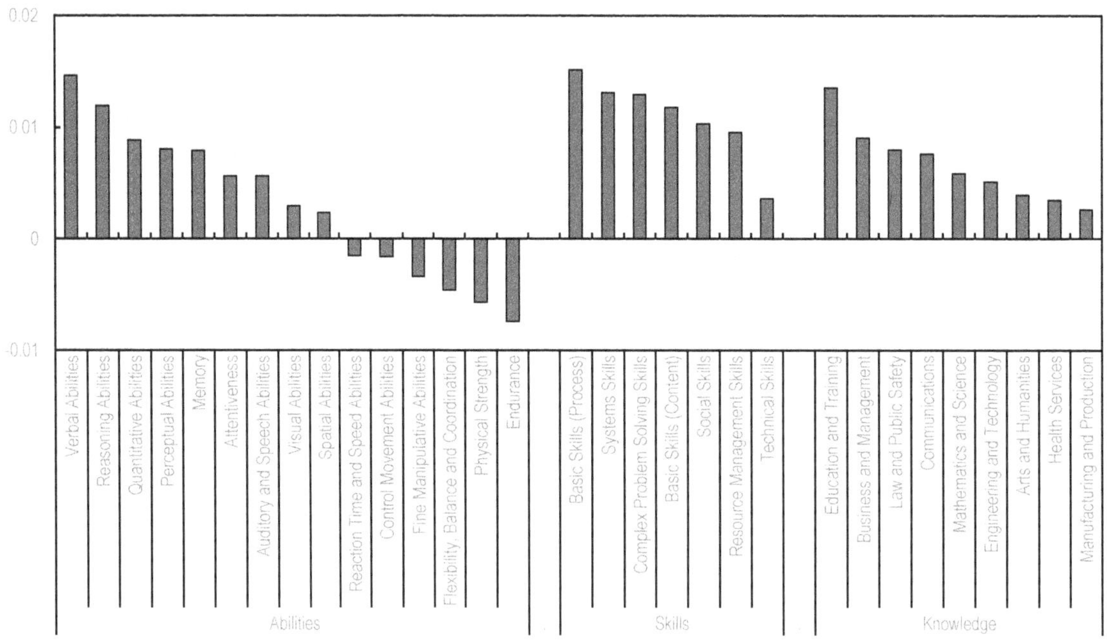

Note: 2016 data
Source: OECD Skills for Jobs Database

At the occupational level, almost all management jobs and more than 50% of jobs in the categories of professionals, technicians and associate professionals, and clerical support workers are in shortage in the South African labour market (Figure 1.6). The fewest jobs in shortage are found among elementary occupations. When looking only at occupations in shortage, Figure 1.6 shows that the intensity of these shortages is strongest for occupations in the professionals category, followed by occupations in the categories of plant and machine operators and assemblers, and skilled agricultural, forestry, fishery, craft and related trades workers.

Figure 1.6. Many high-skill occupations are facing shortages

Share of employment in shortage (left axis) and intensity of the shortages/surpluses (right axis)

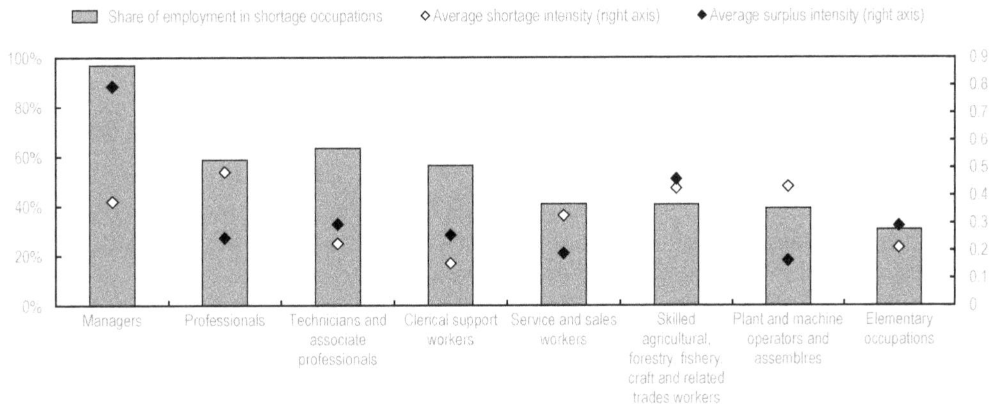

Note: The average shortage intensity is the average of the occupational shortage index among shortage occupations. The average surplus intensity is the average of the absolute value of the occupational shortage index among surplus occupations. Occupations are classified according to the Organising Framework for Occupations.
Source: OECD Skills for Jobs database

The problem of skills shortages has been recognised by the South African government in several strategic documents, and a labour market intelligence system has been set up to analyse skill needs. Multiple policies have been put into place to reduce skills imbalances, including a skills development levy for employers, a subsidy and loan programme for TVET and higher education students and a career guidance system that communicates on labour market needs.[10] The introduction of a Community Education and Training system is another response to the challenge of skills shortages in South Africa. At the same time, by targeting vulnerable adults, the Community Education and Training system has the potential to contribute to lower poverty and inequality.

Notes

[1] Statistics South Africa (StatsSA) breaks down the labour market data into "less than Matric", "Matric", "Graduates" and "Other tertiary". Graduates are individuals who attended a university or college and obtained a post-higher diploma, a bachelor's degree, a post-graduate diploma or an honours, master's or doctoral degree. The group "Other tertiary" comprises people who have attended a Technical Vocational Education and Training (TVET) college or another tertiary institution and obtained a certificate, diploma (with or without matric) or a higher diploma.

[2] Using 2015 population estimates from Statistics South Africa (Statistics South Africa, 2015[18]).

[3] In Brazil, the difference between the share of adults (25-64) and the share of 25-34 year olds with below upper secondary education amounts to 14.6 percentage points. In India and Indonesia, this difference equals 7.3 and 11.2 percentage points, respectively. (OECD, 2017[3])

[4] Data on the share of adults with below lower secondary education are derived from the 2016 South African Labour Force Survey.

[5] In South Africa, Grade 9 students rather than Grade 8 students participate in TIMSS. Their average age is 16.

[6] The World Bank Enterprise Survey limits its definition of training to programmes that have a structured and defined curriculum. This can include classroom work, seminars, lectures, workshops, and audio-visual presentations and demonstrations.

[7] In 2016, around 160 000 students were enrolled in private colleges, including private TVET colleges, private AET centres and private skills development providers. The majority of students in private colleges participate in Nated programmes and Senior Certificate (Amended) programmes.

[8] Data on the age profile of higher education students refers to 2013 and only include public higher education institutions. (Council on Higher Education, 2016[14])

[9] The number of SMEs and cooperatives that receive support from the NSF is projected to decline from 2158 in 2016/17 to 300 in 2020/21.

[10] See OECD (2017[11]) for an extensive review of policies put in place in South Africa to address skills imbalances.

References

Aitchison, J. (2016), "Proxies and perplexities: What is the current state of adult (il)literacy in South Africa?", *Journal of Education*, http://joe.ukzn.ac.za. [2]

B-BBEE Commission (2016), *Broad-Based Black Economic Empowerment Act 53 of 2003 as amended by Act 46 of 2013*, http://bbbeecommission.co.za/wp-content/uploads/2016/09/Consolidated-B-BBEE-Act-2013.pdf (accessed on 25 April 2018). [12]

Council on Higher Education (2016), *2013 Higher Education Data: Participation*, http://www.che.ac.za/focus_areas/higher_education_data/2013/participation (accessed on 20 March 2018). [14]

Department of Higher Education and Training (2016), *Statistics on Post-School Education and Training in South Africa Statistics on Post-School Education and Training in South Africaa*, Department for Higher Education and Training. [9]

DNA Economics (2016), *An analysis of existing post-school education and training expenditure and revenue*, DNA Economics, https://www.gtac.gov.za/perdetail/Vol%202.%20Revenue%20and%20Expenditure%20Review.pdf (accessed on 25 April 2018). [13]

Field, S., P. Musset and J. Álvarez-Galván (2014), *A Skills beyond School Review of South Africa*, OECD Reviews of Vocational Education and Training, OECD Publishing, Paris, http://dx.doi.org/10.1787/9789264223776-en. [10]

Gustafsson, M. (2017), "An update on improvements in schooling outcomes in South Africa", Department for Basic Education. [7]

Lolwana, P., E. Rabe and M. Morakane (2018), "Who accesses adult education and where do they progress to? An exploratory tracer study in community education and training", *LMIP reports*, No. 37, Labour Market Intelligence Parternship, http://www.lmip.org.za/document/who-accesses-adult-education-and-where-do-they-progress-exploratory-tracer-study-community (accessed on 7 November 2018). [8]

National Treasury (2018), *Budget 2018: Estimates of National Expenditure*. [15]

National Treasury (2017), *Budget 2017: Estimates of National Expenditure*. [16]

OECD (2017), *Education at a Glance 2017: OECD Indicators*, OECD Publishing, Paris, https://dx.doi.org/10.1787/eag-2017-en. [3]

OECD (2017), *Getting Skills Right: Skills for Jobs Indicators*, Getting Skills Right, OECD Publishing, Paris, http://dx.doi.org/10.1787/9789264277878-en. [17]

OECD (2017), *Getting Skills Right: South Africa*, Getting Skills Right, OECD Publishing, Paris, http://dx.doi.org/10.1787/9789264278745-en. [11]

Reddy, V. et al. (2015), *Beyond Benchmarks: What twenty years of TIMSS data tell us about South African education*, HSRC, http://www.ipgbook.com. [6]

Simkins, C. (2013), *Performance in the South African Educational System: What do we know?*, Centre for Development & Enterprise. [4]

Statistics South Africa (2015), "Mid-year population estimates", *Statistical release*, No. P0302, https://www.statssa.gov.za/publications/P0302/P03022015.pdf (accessed on 3 July 2018). [18]

StatsSA (2019), *Quarterly Labour Force Survey - Quarter 4: 2018.* [1]

Van Broekhuizen, H., S. Van Der Berg and H. Hofmeyr (2017), "Higher Education Access and Outcomes for the 2008 National Matric Cohort", *LMIP report*, http://www.lmip.org.za/sites/default/files/documentfiles//HSRC%20LMIP%20Report%2030%2024JUL%20WEB.pdf (accessed on 20 March 2018). [5]

Chapter 2. The history and current state of Community Education and Training in South Africa

This chapter looks at the former system of adult (basic) education and training that provided opportunities for South African adults to participate in education at the lower and upper secondary level. It also discusses the existing mass literacy campaign and second chance programme for upper secondary students wanting to obtain the National Senior Certificate. The key legislation and frameworks surrounding the new community education and training system are summarised to provide an overview of the current state of and vision for community education and training in South Africa.

2.1. Adult (basic) education and training

Since the start of democracy in South Africa, adult education featured among the policy priorities of the government.[1] However, it was not until the 2000 Adult Basic Education and Training (ABET) Act that the adult education system was regulated. The ABET Act introduced learning and training programmes at level 1 to 4, with level 4 being equivalent to Grade 9 in the initial education system or NQF level 1 (see Table 2.1, for details on the levels). These ABET programmes are provided in Public Adult Learning Centres (PALCs) (which have recently been renamed as Community Learning Centres) and in registered private learning centres. Adults can obtain a General Education and Training Certificate: Adult Education and Training (GETC: ABET) at the NQF level 1. While ABET enrolment can help individuals prepare for the GETC: ABET, enrolment is not a requirement for taking the exam. According to Umalusi, the council for quality assurance in general and further education and training, around 56 000 GETC: ABET certificates were issued in 2016/2017.

The scope of adult education was later expanded to also include training at the Grade 10 to 12 level (i.e. upper-secondary education), changing its name from ABET to Adult Education and Training (AET). Adults can obtain a Senior Certificate (Amended), which is registered at the NQF level 4 (i.e. the same level as the National Senior Certificate (NSC), generally referred to as Matric).[2] While the Senior Certificate (Amended) is very similar to the NSC, it does not allow graduates to continue to university.[3] In 2016/2017, Umalusi issued just over 66 000 Senior Certificates (Amended).

Table 2.1. Adult Education and Training (AET) levels

AET level	Equivalent school grades	Access to certificate/qualification	NQF level
AET level 1	Grades 1- 3		
AET level 2	Grades 4- 6		
AET level 3	Grades 7- 8		
AET level 4	Grade 9	GETC: ABET	1
Grade 10	Grade 10		2
Grade 11	Grade 11		3
Grade 12	Grade 12	Senior Certificate (Amended)	4

The GETC:ABET and the Senior Certificate (Amended) are expected to be replaced soon by the General Education and Training Certificate for Adults (GETCA) and the National Senior Certificate for Adults (NASCA) respectively. The main difference between the GETCA and its predecessor lies in its curriculum, which will be better targeted towards adult learners. The NASCA introduces similar changes to its curriculum, and will allow graduates to access higher education (provided they obtain the required pass marks). The certificate is also more flexible: Participants may register for any number of subjects per examination sitting, provided they complete the qualification within six years. There are no minimum education requirements[4] for the NASCA, but it is recommended to have a documented Grade 9 pass or a GETCA.[5]

2.2. Basic skills and second chance Matric programmes

The Kha Ri Gude Literacy Campaign managed to substantially reduce illiteracy among adults

As a response to the low skill levels of many South African adults, the South African government launched in 2008 the Kha Ri Gude Literacy Campaign. The campaign is being phased out since the end of 2016/2017. The aim of the campaign was to reduce the illiteracy rate by 50% by 2015 (i.e. reaching 4.7 million people), as such empowering socially disadvantaged people to become self-reliant and able to participate more effectively in the economy. The programme provides 240 hours of training to all participants, free of charge. The focus of the training is to teach people to i) read and write in their mother tongue, ii) use spoken English, and iii) develop a basic number concept and apply arithmetic operations to everyday contexts. At the end of the training, participants should achieve an equivalence of Grade 3 in the basic schooling system (i.e. AET level 1, see Table 2.1). The programme also has a life skills component, which puts emphasis on themes that are central to the participants' socioeconomic context, such as health or income generation. The campaign provides inclusive education, and specific efforts are made to target vulnerable groups, like women, old-age individuals, youth and people living with disabilities. With around 40 000 learning centres across the country, often in informal settings, the campaign has been able to reach learners from rural areas and informal settlements. In the period 2008/09 to 2016/17 the campaign reached almost 4.4 million South Africans (Figure 2.1), 62% of them being female, at a cost of ZAR 4.2 billion.

Figure 2.1. The Kha Ri Gude campaign reached many illiterate South Africans

Number of participants and share of women

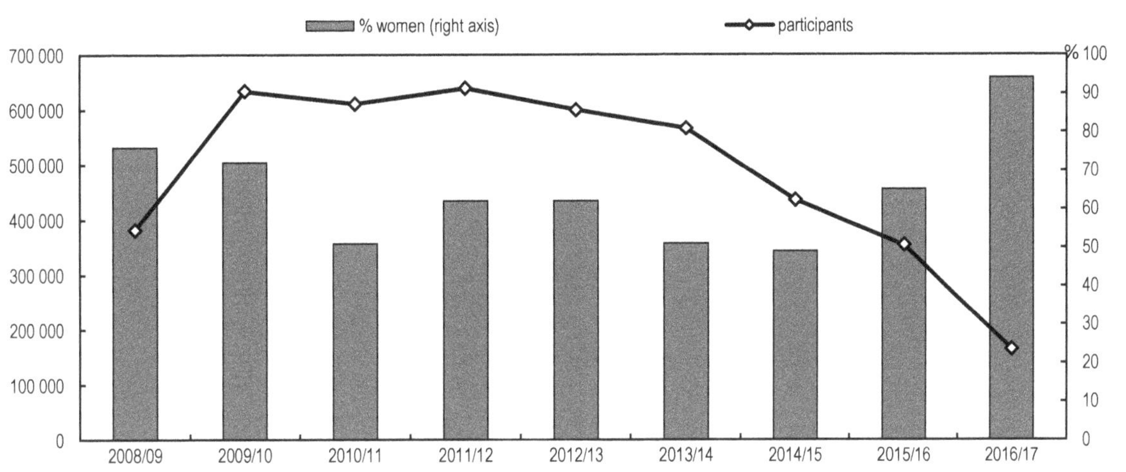

Source: Department of Basic Education (2017[1]; 2017[2]).

The Kha Ri Gude programme relies on volunteers to work as programme educators and facilitators. Annually around 40 000 volunteers were actively working on the programme. Only individuals with at least a Matric qualification are recruited as volunteers, and all volunteers receive basic training related to various aspects of adult education. The volunteers receive a monthly stipend, provided they meet certain criteria (e.g. submitting learner assessment portfolios). In the period 2008/09 to 2016/17 the programme created work opportunities for almost 350 000 volunteers, and 217 of them were awarded Funza Lushaka bursaries to obtain a full teaching qualification.

An extensive monitoring and evaluation system has been set up to ensure the effectiveness of the Kha Ri Gude campaign. Educators are monitored by supervisors, and these supervisors are in turn monitored by coordinators.[6] In addition, participants are continuously assessed in literacy and numeracy, using learner assessment portfolios. These tests are marked by the volunteers, and further moderated and controlled by the supervisors and coordinators. The South African Qualifications Authority (SAQA) furthers verifies a sample of the portfolios to ascertain the general integrity of the marking. Participants who successfully complete their portfolio receive a certificate at AET level 1, and are actively encouraged to register for Adult Education and Training at the primary and lower-secondary level (AET 2-4). (McKay, 2015[3])

The Kha Ri Gude campaign received several national and international awards, including the Unesco Confucius Prize for Literacy, acknowledging the innovative and inclusive character of the programme. The campaign successfully reached out to a large and diverse group of illiterate adults, and the average completion rate is higher than what is generally observed in literacy programmes (McKay, 2015[3]). In addition to helping to eradicate illiteracy, the programme also created work opportunities and income generation for a large number of volunteers, therefore contributing to poverty alleviation. Some negative points were, however, brought to light by a performance evaluation of the Auditor General of South Africa, including fruitless and wasteful expenditure, part of which was the result of fraudulent behaviour of a number of volunteer educators.

A second chance programme has been put in place to support students retaking the Matric examination

Over the last ten years, the National Senior Certificate (NSC or Matric) exam pass rate in South Africa increased significantly. In 2017, 75.1% of students who took the NSC exam passed it, compared to 65.2% in 2007. In an effort to further increase the pass rate, and hence the number of students that could potentially advance to further education and training, the Department for Basic Education launched the Second Chance programme in 2016. The programme provides free online learning materials, radio and television broadcast lessons, as well as face-to-face classes. The latter are only provided in areas with a sufficient number of students. The programme is available for four types of students:

- *Supplementary exam candidates:* Students who failed at most two subjects during the NSC exam are allowed to retake those subjects in a supplementary exam. These exams take place three months after the initial NSC exam. In 2017, almost 125 000 students enrolled for the supplementary exam, but only 62% of them actually participated. The pass rate was low, with only 18% individuals taking the exam also obtaining the certificate ((Parliamentary Monitoring Group, 2017[4])).
- *Progressed learners taking the multiple exam opportunity:* Students who progress to the next grade without fulfilling all the promotion requirements are referred to as progressed learners.[7] Progressed learners in grade 12 who perform weakly throughout the year are allowed the Multiple Examinations Opportunity, which gives them the possibility to spread their NSC subjects over two exam periods (November and June). In the first exam session, a minimum of three subjects must be taken. There were just over 107 000 progressed learners among the 802 000 Matric candidates in 2007.

- *Senior Certificate (Amended) exam candidates*: Adults can obtain the Senior Certificate (Amended), a certificate at the same level as the NSC. See Section 2.1 for details.
- *NSC part-time exam candidates*: Students who took the NSC exam for the first time over the previous three years and want to repeat one or more subjects, may register as a part-time candidate for the NSC examinations. Part-time candidates may not take more than six subjects in one examination round. This option allows students who failed one or more subject in their matric exam to repeat these subjects the next year, and combine the results from the two examination rounds. In 2017, 117 000 part-time candidates took the Matric exam.

Until 2016, a similar small-scale second change Matric Rewrite programme was run by the National Youth Development Agency, which recorded 21 000 participants over six years.

2.3. Building a Community Education and Training system

Acknowledging that the provision of education and training opportunities for adults and young people who dropped out of school before completing was inadequate, the Department for Higher Education and Training's (DHET) Green Paper for Post-school Education and Training articulated the idea of creating a community education and training system (Department of Higher Education and Training, 2012[5]). The Green Paper argues that the Adult Education and Training (AET) system does not satisfy the needs of adults interested not only in completing their schooling, but also in acquiring labour market or sustainable livelihood skills. At the same time, the AET system does not harness the potential for development and social cohesion that exists in some community and popular education initiatives. To address these issues, the Green Paper proposed to develop a Community Education and Training (CET) system that would absorb the public adult learning centres (PALCs) and gradually expand to other skills programmes.

The ideas from the Green Paper were, after public consultation, further formalised in the 2013 White Paper (Department of Higher Education and Training, 2013[6]), which sets a goal of 1 million students in CET institutions by 2030 (compared to 265 000 students in public adult learning centres in 2011). The main features of the CET system are described as:

- Role: Facilitate a cycle of lifelong learning in communities by enabling the development of skills (including literacy, numeracy and vocational skills) to enhance personal, social, family and employment experiences. Assist community organisations and institutions, local government, individuals and local businesses to work together to develop their communities by building on existing knowledge and skills.
- Setup: Multi-campus institutions that cluster the PALCs. Other campuses will be added where necessary based on enrolments and programmes.
- Curriculum: CET institutions will build on the current offerings of the PALCs to expand vocational and skills-development programmes and non-formal programmes. Non-formal programmes will be geared to the needs and desires of local communities and their organisations, including community-based cooperatives and businesses

- Cooperation with community institutions: CET colleges and their campuses should make an effort to draw on the strengths of the non-formal sector (particularly their community responsiveness and focus on citizen and social education), in order to strengthen and expand popular citizen and community education. They may enter into partnerships with community-owned or private institutions.
- Teacher quality: A qualifications policy for adult educators will be put in place that describes appropriate qualifications and sets minimum standards for these qualifications. Universities and TVET colleges will be supported to develop capacity to train adult educators.
- Funding: The DHET will provide the core funding of the colleges, including for core permanent teaching and administrative staff, and this has to be complemented by funds from SETAs, the National Skills Fund (NSF) and the private sector where appropriate and available. CET colleges may charge fees for some of the programmes that they provide, especially for those funded by SETAs, the NSF or the private sector. In general, as far as possible, youth and adults attending CET colleges will be fully funded, whether by the DHET or from other sources.

In April 2015 the first nine CET colleges were opened, one in each province, clustering the existing 3 276 PALCs. The PALCs were renamed as Community Learning Centres (CLCs). The nine colleges serve as administrative hubs, whereas the CLCs are delivery sites of CET. The long-term goals is to have a CET college in each of the 52 district municipalities, and a CLC in each of the 226 local municipalities. The CET system forms a third pillar in the post-school education and training system (see Figure 2.2).

Since the publication of the White Paper on Post-School Education and Training, the DHET has released (draft) policies and frameworks on a range of topics related to the CET system, including curriculum development, staffing norms, monitoring and evaluation, and student support services (see Annex A for a full overview).

In July 2017, the Ministerial Committee on the review of the funding frameworks of TVET Colleges and CET colleges published a report on the funding framework for CET. It concludes that the current adult education and training system is of very poor quality, and that the current mode of operation and available funding does not allow for significant quality improvements. A steady process of reform and incremental growth is needed, starting with a proper holding operation and a new CET implementation plan. The main recommendations from the report are described in Box 2.1.

Figure 2.2. The post-school education and training system

Institutions, programmes and student enrolment

Community Education and Training (CET)	Technical and Vocational Education and Training (TVET)	Higher Education
Institutions	**Institutions**	**Institutions**
9 CET Colleges (administrative hubs), with 3 276 delivery sites (Community Learning Centres)	50 Public TVET colleges, with 250 campuses	26 Public Higher Education Institutions (HEIs), i.e. Universities and Technical Universities
Private institutions	Private institutions	123 Private Higher Education institutions
Programmes	**Programmes**	**Programmes**
AET 1-4	NATED (N1-N6)	Undergraduate degrees, certificates and diplomas
Grade 10-12	National Certificate Vocational (NCV)	Post-graduate (below master's level)
Occupational/Skills programmes	Occupational/Skills programmes	Master's degrees
Non-formal programmes		Doctoral degrees
Students	**Students**	**Students**
273 431 students in public CET institutions	705 397 in public TVET colleges	975 867 students in public HEIs
61 118 students in private institutions	107 793 students in private institutions	167 408 students in private HEIs

SETA-supported workplace-based learning	
Programmes	**Students**
Internships	17 216 learners (100% job-seekers)
Learnerships & apprenticeships	101 447 learners (63% job-seekers)

Note: Official data on enrolment in private colleges is not split into CET and TVET. The allocation of students to CET and TVET in this table is done based on the qualification category of the students in private colleges. Students in Nated, NCV and occupational programmes are allocated to the TVET sector, students in AET-type of programmes are allocated to the CET sector. Part of the students in SETA-supported workplace-based learning programmes will also be enrolled in public or private TVET institutions, and will hence be double-counted in this overview.
Source: Department for Higher Education and Training (2016[7]).

Box 2.1. The Ministerial Committees' recommendations on funding the CET system

In light of the forthcoming National Plan for Post-Secondary Education and Training, a Ministerial Committee on the review of the funding frameworks of TVET and CET was put in place. The poor outcomes from TVET and CET colleges have often been attributed to the fact that funding allocations have not kept pace with the increased number of students. The Ministerial Council concludes that more resources need to be mobilised from a variety of sectors in order for these colleges to play a more useful role in society. Their recommendations for the CET sector include:

- *Legislation*: Once a sound conceptual model of the CET sector is developed it should be piloted and then a comprehensive Adult and CET Act should be developed (which is not simply a clone of the legislation relating to TVET Colleges.)
- *Structural reform and funding:*
  - o CET institutions should move towards a more community-oriented rather than

school-based approach. There should be no admission criteria ensuring access to all who want to attend.

- There needs to be a framework for institutional growth with due attention paid to the need for considerable funding for the effective development of this sector, as well as to more effective use of existing infrastructure and to its expansion.
- Communities, local government and civil society bodies must be involved in the conceptualisation and development of the local CET institutions, including enrolment planning and the qualifications and programmes that should be offered, all within the context of the development of the regions where the institution is based.
- A dedicated high level CET sector development support team should be set up to develop and monitor the implementation plans for each new CET institution and simultaneously undertake the necessary demographic and demand analyses to justify investment in CET institutions in those particular localities.

- *Setting the level of funding*: The overall budget should be increased as fast as possible to at least 3% of the national education budget as an interim measure and certain percentages of the budget should be ring-fenced for personnel costs (including coordination), curriculum and materials, maintenance and monitoring and evaluation. Materials development should be a priority in the initial year or two. Building the capacity of the institutions to handle an increase in funding needs to be factored in.
- *Use of private and public facilities*: Given the low likelihood of massive funding for new infrastructure in the near future, the state should encourage the use of spare capacity in public college and university facilities. Similarly, private non-profit facilities could also be used on fair contractual terms. In addition, the DHET should negotiate with municipalities to identify available facilities for this purpose, potentially in cooperation with the South African Local Government Association. There is also scope for the use of schools that have closed down.
- Incorporation of the *Kha Ri Gude* structure into the CET system.

General recommendations include substantially increasing spending on the TVET and CET system, and limiting staff costs to 70% of the total budget. The report also highlights the importance of differentiation between TVET and CET colleges to avoid duplication.

Source: Ministerial Committee on the review of funding frameworks of TVET and CET colleges (2017[8])

Notes

[1] Before and during the apartheid regime, adult education was mainly organised informally, usually at the initiative of NGOs. See Aitchison (2003[9]) for a detailed overview of adult education in South Africa in the 20th century.

[2] Before the introduction of the National Senior Certificate (NSC) in 2014, adults could participate in the National Certificate examinations. With the introduction of the NSC, which is limited to individuals of at most 20 years old, a gap was created for adult learners wanting to obtain an NQF level 4 qualification. This gap is currently (but temporarily) filled by the Senior Certificate (Amended), in anticipation of a new senior certificate targeted at adult learners.

[3] As an interim measure, adults who obtained the Senior Certificate (Amended) can get an age exemption for university access.

[4] There are a few minimum requirements that are unrelated to educational attainment: participants must be at least 18 years old, hold a valid South African document of identification and may not be enrolled at a public or independent school

[5] Individuals who hold other NQF level 2 or 3 qualifications with languages and mathematics as fundamentals also fulfil the minimum prior learning recommendations.

[6] Each supervisor monitors ten educators, and each co-ordinator monitors 20 supervisors.

[7] In the South African education system, students may not spend more than four years in any particular education phase, and can therefore only fail one grade once. After that, learners are advanced to the next grade even if they fail the promotion requirements. There are, however, some minimum requirements in terms of attendance and performance.

References

Aitchison, J. (2003), "Struggle and compromise: a history of South African adult education from 1960 to 2001", *Journal of Education* 29, pp. 125-178. [9]

Department of Basic Education (2017), *Annual Report 2016/17*, https://www.education.gov.za/Portals/0/Documents/Reports/DBE%20Annual%20Report%202017.pdf?ver=2017-09-26-090956-673 (accessed on 23 March 2018). [2]

Department of Basic Education (2017), *Kha Ri Gude Mass Literacy Campaign: 2008 to 2016/2017*. [1]

Department of Higher Education and Training (2016), *Statistics on Post-School Education and Training in South Africa Statistics on Post-School Education and Training in South Africaa*, Department for Higher Education and Training. [7]

Department of Higher Education and Training (2013), *White Paper for Post-School Education and Training*. [6]

Department of Higher Education and Training (2012), *Green Paper for Post-School Education and Training*. [5]

McKay, V. (2015), "Measuring and monitoring in the South African Kha Ri Gude mass literacy campaign", *International Review of Education*, Vol. 61, pp. 365-397, http://dx.doi.org/10.1007/s11159-015-9495-8. [3]

Ministerial Committee on the review of the funding frameworks of TVET Colleges and CET colleges (2017), *Information Report and Appendices for presentation to Minister B.E. Nzimande, M.P.*. [8]

Parliamentary Monitoring Group (2017), *NSC 2016 examination results; Examination merge; Annual National Assessment (ANA) remodelling | PMG*, https://pmg.org.za/committee-meeting/24590/ (accessed on 29 March 2018). [4]

Chapter 3. What should be the role of Community Education and Training?

This chapter zooms in on the role that community education and training could play in the South African post-school education system. The current adult education system only provides for adult basic education, as enshrined in the South African constitution. This chapter explores what other types of training could be provided by the community education and training system, and who should be the main target audience. The chapter provides good practice example from other countries and concrete actions that can be taken to advance and position the community education and training system in South Africa.

3.1. Background

Lifelong learning activities for adults generally take three forms: formal, non-formal and informal learning (Desjardins, 2017[1]). Formal adult education and training usually leads to an official qualification, and can be general in nature (e.g. adults in higher education or adults in second chance secondary education), but also vocationally oriented. These types of programmes are generally provided by formal education and training institutions (e.g. TVET colleges, universities). Non-formal training does not necessarily lead to widely recognised qualifications, but still constitutes structured and organised learning opportunities. This can include seminars, workshops or on-the-job training activities. Non-formal training is often provided by employers, but also by public and private education and training institutions, non-profit organisations and trade unions. Informal learning, on the other hand, is generally less deliberate and unstructured, and includes learning by doing and learning from others. Because of its unstructured nature, informal learning is not delivered by a specific provider. Across OECD countries, adults participate much more in non-formal and informal learning activities than in formal education and training (Fialho, Quintini and Vandeweyer, 2019[2])

Adults face multiple barriers when it comes to participation in lifelong learning activities. In OECD countries, the main reason for adults not to participate or participate more in training is because they are too busy at work, followed by childcare and family responsibility and training being too expensive (OECD, 2017[3]). Interestingly, among individuals who do not participate in training, the large majority also has no interest in participating. The lack of interest and other barriers to participation are generally bigger for low-skilled adults (OECD, 2019[4]). Evidence shows that it is hard for adults to improve their skills mid-life. Often those concerned will have done badly at school, and have a very negative perception of education and learning; they may lack awareness of their deficiencies, and even if aware, be embarrassed to admit it (in respect of reading difficulties for example). Initial motivation is therefore a serious obstacle (Musset, 2015[5]; Windisch, 2015[6]). Engaging adults, especially low skilled ones, requires sensitivity to the different ways in which they might be motivated and how they might want to learn. Some adult learners are highly dependent on teachers for structure and guidance, while others prefer to manage their own learning. Some may be motivated to learn because of some specific objective, like getting a new job or helping their children with homework, others may want to learn out of curiosity. Adults typically prefer to learn what is meaningful to them (see Windisch (2015[6]) for a review of the literature).

In light of the difficulties to engage adults to participate in lifelong learning, it is of crucial importance that the training opportunities available for adults are useful and targeted to their needs and circumstances. In OECD countries, the large majority of adults participating in adult learning opportunities do so for job-related reasons, such as to do their job better or improve their career prospects (OECD, 2019[4]). Many types of training programmes can be job-related, including vocational programmes, but also basic skills programmes. Importantly, adults who want to improve their skills to have better labour market outcomes must clearly understand the benefits of different types of programmes. To improve access to lifelong learning opportunities, adults need to understand the different types of education and training institutions that exist and the programmes they offer. This is typically the task of career guidance and counselling, which generally requires the following competences (Musset and Mytna Kurekova, 2018[7]):

- Good knowledge of education systems, labour markets, careers and learning opportunities, and the capacity to identify and use further relevant sources of information to provide more specific career advice to individuals.
- The capacity to identify the interests, aptitudes and objectives of potential learners and together develop education and career choice solutions which are both realistic and meet their needs in the context of changing labour markets.
- Readiness to continuously analyse changes in the labour market and importantly adjust professional counselling (OECD, 2010[8]).

Community Education and Training is one type of institutional setup that can deliver lifelong learning opportunities to adults. According to Unesco (2012[9]), the role of community learning centres is to provide opportunities for lifelong learning to all people in the local community. The main functions of these centres are to provide i) education and training, ii) community information and resource services, iii) community development activities, and iv) coordination and networking. The next sections of this chapter discuss the different programmes and services that can be offered in CET institutions in South Africa, with a focus on education and training (second chance, vocational and non-formal) and information and guidance. The services provided can go beyond the areas discussed in this section, and the offer should respond to the needs and preferences of the community (see Chapter 5 for details on how to ensure alignment with community needs). As pointed out by Lolwana, Rabe and Morakane (2018[10]), students in CET need a lot more support in order to succeed than the traditional post-school student, including financial support, childcare and health care, retention plans and extracurricular activities. Substantial additional capacity will be needed for the CET system to be able to provide all these different programmes and services. In light of the current and foreseen capacity constraints, the expansion of the CET role can only be done gradually, taking into account capacities and needs of the different CET institutions and the target audience they serve.

3.2. Second chance programmes

Basic skills programmes & primary and lower secondary education for adults with low foundational skills

The key function of the current CET system, as inherited from the AET system, is to deliver adult basic education (i.e. AET level 1-4, with completion equivalent to NQF 1 or Grade 9). Primary and lower secondary education and basic skills programmes should continue to be an essential component of CET in South Africa, especially given that 7.5 million adults in South Africa did not finish Grade 9. These types of programmes help individuals gain access to further education and training opportunities. In some countries, the provision of literacy and basic skill programmes was the starting point for the development of a diversified community education and training system (see Box 3.1).

The right to basic education is part of South Africa's constitution (section 29(1)): "Everyone has the right to a basic education, including adult basic education". Grade 9 (or NQF 1) is the minimum requirement for programmes in TVET colleges and for occupational qualifications. Giving adults the opportunity to participate in adult basic education does therefore not only equip them with the basic skills that are essential for everyday life, it also provides them with the opportunity to advance in further education and training.

Box 3.1. Community Learning Centres in Morocco:From literacy training for women to a diversified offer of learning opportunities

Acknowledging that low literacy rates hamper socio-economic development, the Moroccan government has made the fight against illiteracy one of its top priorities in the last two decades. A national survey showed that in 2006, 38.5% of adults in Morocco were illiterate, and that the problem was particularly pressing for women (46.8%) and in rural areas (54.4%). Following the government's commitment to reduce illiteracy, including the adoption of a National Literacy Strategy in 2004, the number of beneficiaries of literacy programmes increased substantially (from 286 000 in 2002 to 730 000 in 2012).

As part of the literacy strategy, a pilot programme was set up in two provinces with the aim to forge a link between literacy and the socio-economic integration of women who have recently acquired basic literacy skills. The programme involved the creation of four community education centres, run by the communities themselves. These centres were provided with equipment and managers were selected and trained. The centres are accommodated by associations or networks of associations, and have their own activity programmes based on community needs. The participants receive training to refresh and reinforce their literacy and numeracy skills, but also pre-vocational training (based on the interests of the participants and the economic opportunities available in the local area). After the pre-vocational training, participants have the option to pursue in-depth technical training to foster income-generating activities.

By 2017, the number of community education centres increased to around 200, spread across different provinces. An evaluation of the centres showed that they offer a wide variety of training opportunities, including literacy and post-literacy training, professional training (e.g. sewing, hairdressing) and workshops and meetings on awareness-raising topics. Additionally, many centres provide support for small economic projects and the establishment of cooperatives, but also early childhood care facilities to facilitate participation of mothers with young children.

Source: Direction de la Lutte Contre l'Analphabétisme (2012[11]), UNESCO Institute for Lifelong Learning (2013[12]), Avramovska, Hirsch and Schmidt-Behlau (2017[13]).

Among the group of adults without lower secondary education, some did not participate at all in education or participated only for a very brief time. These individuals might lack the very basic skills that are needed to participate in second chance primary and lower secondary education. For these adults, basic skill training would be required, as provided by the Kha Ri Gude campaign (which is currently managed by the Department of Basic Education (DBE)). The campaign reached its objective of reducing by half the number of illiterate adults in South Africa and is being phased out. However, this means that there is still a large group of illiterate individuals in need of this type of training. Providing adults with the opportunity to develop basic literacy and numeracy skills would give them the chance to advance into second chance primary and lower secondary education and improve their education and career pathways. The CET system should acquire the Kha Ri Gude materials for literacy training of CET students, and develop similar adapted and integrated learning materials for AET Levels 1 to 4.

Approaches that gives interesting results for adults are 'contextualised', which means that they identify and address weaknesses in basic skills in a wider context – such as the search for a job or an adult vocational programme. Basic skills acquisition is often embedded in occupational skill programmes, but also programmes such as family literacy (see Windisch (2015[6]) for a review of the evidence). It has been argued that this approach has many advantages. First, it is easier to engage and retain low-skilled adult learners who have negative feelings about 'traditional classroom' numeracy and literacy programmes. Second, it can help retain adult learners, positively change their attitudes towards further education and training, improve their self-confidence and parenting and employability skills, and achieve literacy and numeracy and/or vocational qualifications. Third, basic skills linked to an occupational skill are more likely to be sustained through use in the occupation. The same is true of basic skills linked to practical non-work requirements of everyday life, such as financial literacy. Many countries have therefore championed the approach. But for all its merits, it is hard to deliver effective contextual learning, especially because of the organisational challenges in having literacy and numeracy teachers work together with vocational teachers in a coordinated way (Kuczera, Field and Windisch, 2015[14]).

Recommended action steps

Table 3.1 provides some possible action steps that could be taken to implement and improve basic skills programmes and second chance primary and lower secondary education in CET. For each action, the most relevant stakeholders concerned are listed. The list of stakeholders is not exhaustive, and cooperation between different stakeholders is encouraged. The actions focus on the short- and medium-term, and a more ambitious action plan could be developed for the longer term in line with the vision for CET from the DHET's strategic documents.

Table 3.1. Actions steps for basic skills programmes and second chance primary and lower secondary education

Steps and relevant stakeholders

Action steps	Main stakeholders
Set-up a joint DBE and DHET basic skills task team to discuss the key lessons from the Kha Ri Gude campaign.	DHET, DBE
Take over the Kha Ri Gude learning materials from the DBE to provide basic skills training in CET institutions	DHET, DBE
Design a basic skills programme to be delivered in CET institutions, building on the Kha Ri Gude campaign and insights from the basic skills task team, and optimally using the Kha Ri Gude materials	DHET, DBE, NGOs, Quality Councils
Communicate widely about the continuation of Kha Ri Gude (albeit potentially under a new name and form) in CET institutions	DHET, DBE, CLCs, CET Colleges,
Better encourage and support students completing basic skills programmes to progress into second chance primary and lower secondary education	DBE, CLCs
Develop learning materials for second chance primary and lower secondary education that provide an integrated approach to basic adult education, incorporating life skills. Use the basic skills task team to learn from the experiences of Kha Ri Gude	DHET
Implement the GETCA as soon as possible, and make sure it truly reflects the needs of adult learners in terms of curriculum content and flexibility	DHET, Umalusi

Note: DHET: Department for Higher Education and Training; DBE: Department of Basic Education; CLC: Community Learning Centre.

Upper secondary education for adults wanting to obtain the Senior Certificate

High dropout rates after Grade 9 and a significant number of people who do not pass the National Senior Certificate exam, mean that many students leave initial education without an upper secondary degree (i.e. Matric) (see Chapter 1). Nonetheless, an upper secondary degree is very valuable in the South African labour market: given the large pool of available (unemployed) labour, employers are increasingly requiring an upper secondary degree when looking for candidates (even for jobs for which an upper secondary degree is not necessarily required). In addition, a Matric degree gives access to further education opportunities. Even for TVET programmes at lower NQF-levels (i.e. 2 to 4), opportunities are more limited for individuals without a Matric, as colleges prefer to grant the available spaces to individuals with higher levels of educational attainment.

Many Community Learning Centres are currently providing Grade 12 training courses, and a large (and growing) share of students in the CET system are enrolled in these Grade 12 programmes. At the same time, the Department for Basic Education has just started its new Second Chance Matric programme that provides learning materials and face-to-face classes for people taking another chance at the National Senior Certificate (or at the Senior Certificate (Amended)) (see Chapter 2). It should be guaranteed that people who obtain the Senior Certificate (Amended) or its successor, the NASCA certificate (see Chapter 2), have easy access to further education opportunities.

Second chance upper secondary education should remain at the heart of CET, as it gives individuals the opportunity to obtain the valuable Matric certificate that increases their career opportunities, and opens up a range of different pathways into further education and training. Evidence from a sample of Community Learning Centres shows that the main aspiration of CET students is further education (Lolwana, Rabe and Morakane, 2018[10]). As for basic skills and lower-secondary programmes, upper-secondary CET provision should ideally incorporate life skills into the teaching materials, in an effort to provide integrated learning but also to be closer to the adults' daily realities. Overlap between CET and the DBE's Second Chance Matric programme should be avoided as much as possible, and ideally the face-to-face classes from the Second Chance Matric programme would also be delivered in CET institutions.

Individuals taking part in second chance education with the goal to advance into TVET colleges could benefit from additional support to prepare them for vocational education. Information about different vocational careers could help them make informed education choices, and employability training and information on how to look for workplace-based learning opportunities could benefit the successful completion of their TVET training. In Germany, a pre-apprenticeship programme is available for students with low educational attainment wanting to enter the dual vocational system (see Box 3.2).

Recommended action steps

Table 3.2 provides some possible action steps that could be taken to implement and improve second chance upper secondary education in CET. For each action step, the most relevant stakeholders concerned are listed. The list of stakeholders is not exhaustive, and cooperation between different stakeholders is encouraged. The actions steps focus on the short- and medium-term, and a more ambitious action plan could be developed for the longer term in line with the vision for CET from the DHET's strategic documents.

Table 3.2. Actions steps for second chance upper secondary education

Action steps and relevant stakeholders

Action steps	Main stakeholders
Introduce the NASCA certificate as soon as possible, ensuring it is flexible and has the same value as the National Senior Certificate (NSC). Clarify the rules around who can (re-)take the NSC exam and who can take the NASCA exam.	DHET, DBE, Umalusi
Engage closely with the DBE on their Second Chance Matric programme. Make sure that potential students understand the difference between Grade 12 in CET and the DBE's Second Chance Matric programme. Make the DBE's Second Chance Matric learning materials and face-to-face classes available in CET institutions.	DHET, DBE
Develop teaching and learning materials adapted to adults (as for second chance primary and lower secondary education) and ensure sufficient flexibility. Make sure a career guidance component is included in the curriculum.	DHET
Reduce dropouts in upper secondary education by fully developing TVET NQF 2-4 as an alternative pathway to the academic route (Grade 10-12). This will lower the need for second chance education. Investment in TVET should be done to ensure sufficient places for non-Matric holders.	DHET, DBE

Note: DHET: Department for Higher Education and Training; DBE: Department of Basic Education.

Short remedial courses can help adults close basic skills gaps

As CET will expand to also offer vocational skills programmes (see below), it will become important to ensure that participants in these programmes also have access to remedial or bridging courses to freshen up or improve some essential literacy and numeracy skills. The skills of these participants might not be up to standard with workplace and further education requirements. At the same time, these adults are potentially not interested in participating in full academic second chance programmes (at the lower- or upper-secondary level) and they might already possess the very basic literacy skills targeted in literacy programmes. For these adults, short remedial courses can be useful to ensure that they have the foundational skills needed to participate in vocational programmes, but also to facilitate their progression into the labour market or further education. The need for this type of remedial courses was confirmed by a number of CET students, who pointed out that gaps in general and foundational education make it difficult for learners to access skills quickly and effectively (Lolwana, Rabe and Morakane, 2018[10]).

Research shows that many people cannot adequately assess their own literacy and numeracy weaknesses. Data from various cohort studies in the United Kingdom show that many people with weak basic skills do not recognise their own difficulties, particularly in numeracy. Once people are aware of weaknesses in their basic skills, they tend to want to improving them (Bynner and Parsons, 2006[15]). Given all the difficulties of persuading adults who may need help with numeracy and literacy to come forward, an effective approach could be to screen for foundation skills in the context of vocational programmes offered in CET institutions. The materials and expertise developed within the context of the Kha Ri Gude campaign could be helpful for designing these foundational skills screening tools. Screening for basic skills gaps needs to be handled sensitively, so that it is not seen as a barrier to entry and does not demoralise potential learners. A similar approach is taken in community colleges in the United States, which offer developmental (or remedial) education following a basic skills entry test (Kuczera and Field, 2013[16]).

Box 3.2. Pre-vocational training in Germany

In Germany, the dual vocational system is an important component of vocational education and training. In the dual system, students combine school-based vocational learning with company-based learning (apprenticeships). Dual vocational learning at the secondary education level does not require any qualifications, but companies often require at least lower secondary education from their apprentices. To help students without lower secondary education qualifications access apprenticeship opportunities, a pre-vocational training year (*Berufsvorbereitungsjahr*) is made available.

The one-year program at a full-time vocational school offers general education as well as basic occupational training. Additionally, there is guidance helping the students make future career choices. Successful graduates of the pre-vocational training year are awarded a lower secondary school leaving certificate (at the *Hauptschule* level). After completion of the pre-vocational training year, students can search for apprenticeships, or they can continue with a basic vocational training year (*Berufsgrundbildungsjahr*). This programme is open to everyone with a lower secondary degree, and offers general education and practical basic job-specific training, at a higher level than the pre-vocational programme. Students can choose between several occupational fields. Completion of the programme can reduce the duration of a subsequent apprenticeship.

In 2016/17, around 121 000 students started the pre-vocational training year and an additional 6 800 started the basic vocational training year (full-time). The number of students in the pre-vocational training year has been on the rise, with the number of students increasing by 129% since 2014/15. This recent strong growth in overall participation can be entirely attributed to non-German students, who represented two thirds of total participants in 2016/17. Evidence suggests that the pre-vocational training programmes serve as a stepping-stone to enter vocational education mainly for individuals with the lowest qualification levels, but also that additional support is needed for disadvantaged students. Recent data show that around 60% of participants in transition measures (including the pre-vocational training year and the basic vocational training year, but also other transition options) continue into vocational education.

Source: Autorengruppe Bildungsberichterstattung (2018[17]); Beicht (2009[18]); Eichhorst, Wozny and Cox (2015[19]); Erban (2010[20]); Statistisches Bundesamt (2018[21])

Recommended action steps

Table 3.3 provides some possible action steps that could be taken to implement and improve remedial course in CET. For each action step, the most relevant stakeholders concerned are listed. The list of stakeholders is not exhaustive, and cooperation between different stakeholders is encouraged. The actions steps focus on the short- and medium-term, and a more ambitious action plan could be developed for the longer term in line with the vision for CET from the DHET's strategic documents.

Table 3.3. Actions steps for short remedial

Action steps and relevant stakeholders

Action steps	Main stakeholders
Develop tools, using the expertise of the Kha Ri Gude campaign, to screen for weaknesses in basic skills upon entry in certain CET programmes, and offer targeted help for those who need it.	DHET, DBE
Develop modules of basic skills training at different levels that can be combined flexibly.	DHET, DBE, Quality councils
Promote these short remedial courses among participants in vocational skills programmes.	CLCs

Note: DHET: Department of Higher Education and Training; DBE: Department of Basic Education; CLC: Community Learning Centre.

3.3. Vocational skills programmes

Adults without upper secondary education do not necessarily want to participate in purely academic training programmes to obtain a lower or upper secondary qualification. For many adults the reason for participating in training activities is to improve their labour market outcomes, and improved literacy and numeracy skills may on their own not provide sufficient impetus to change or improve careers. Exploratory research on a sample of CET students shows that the desire to get a (better) job is the second most important reason for participating in CET (after wanting to study further). For this reason, adults should have easy access to vocational training opportunities. Currently, TVET colleges are mainly providing long-term programmes (Nated and NCV) that are not targeted to adult learners. Occupational programmes only represent a very small part in the overall TVET offering, with only 2% of all students in TVET colleges enrolled in these programmes (Department of Higher Education and Training, 2016[22]). At the same time, as pointed out by Field, Musset and Álvarez-Galván (2014[23]), TVET programmes are rarely organised as distance education or on a part-time basis. Ensuring that adults have access to vocational training opportunities can be achieved by making programmes in TVET colleges more flexible, and by offering vocational programmes adapted to the needs of adult learners in the CET system. This would echo the approach taken in other countries.

Some Community Learning Centres are already providing vocational skills programmes, such as welding, auto-mechanics, sewing, baking and computer skills, but they remain a minority. Some of these programmes are accredited, meaning that they deliver NQF (part-) qualifications (usually at level 2 or 3). Many different types of vocational skills programmes exist in South Africa, and the difference between them is not always easy to understand. Box 3.3 provides more information about the three main types of vocational skills programmes: vocational, occupational and skills programmes.

While the provision of vocational skills programmes in CET is clearly of high value, overlaps with the programmes offered in TVET colleges within close geographical proximity should be avoided as much as possible, especially when resources are limited. Ideally, vocational skills programmes in CET are short-term, to be easily accessible to adults but also to allow sufficient flexibility to respond to community needs (see Chapter 5). Over time, some TVET programmes could be made available in the CET system, provided they are adapted to the needs of adults. Importantly, to avoid unnecessary investment in equipment and use existing knowledge and experience as much as possible, the CET system should cooperate closely with TVET colleges in their neighbourhood.

Box 3.3. Vocational, occupational and skills programmes in South Africa

Vocational qualifications

There are two types of vocational qualifications in South Africa, delivered in TVET colleges: National Certificate Vocational (NCV) and Nated:

- The NCV programmes are available at levels 2 to 4 of the National Qualifications Framework (NQF). The programmes include three general and four vocational subjects. Successful students receive a certificate after levels 2 and 3, and the National Certificate (Vocational) after completing level 4. The NCV has a compulsory practical component, which can be offered in a real or simulated workplace environment.
- Nated programmes are available from level N1 to N6, with N1 to N3 corresponding to NQF level 2-4. The N6 certificate only leads to a national N diploma at NQF level 5 upon completion of 18 months or two years of relevant work experience. The business and services programmes are only available at level N4-N6 and are open to Matric graduates. Other N4-N6 programmes are also open to N3 graduates. Individuals who want to enter the labour market after N2 or N3 need to take a trade test, for which workplace experience is a pre-requisite. The Nated programmes are purely vocationally oriented, and are generally shorter than the NCV programmes. The Nated programmes in themselves do not contain a practical component, and therefore the trade tests and national N diploma require proof of outside work experience.

When the NCV was introduced in 2007, it was meant to gradually replace the N-programmes. Today, however, the majority of TVET students are still enrolled in Nated programmes: In 2016, 177 000 students were enrolled in NCV programmes, compared to 492 000 in N-programmes.

Occupational qualifications

An Occupational Qualification is a qualification associated to a trade, occupation or profession resulting from work-based learning. Occupational qualifications make work experience an important part of learning, and they can be obtained through TVET colleges, SETA learnerships, private providers and colleges, and industry. Over 200 occupational qualifications are registered in the NQF (the occupational qualifications sub-framework). There is considerable variation in the level and length of the programmes, with programmes available on NQF levels 2 to 8 and credits ranging between 28 (forecourt attendant, NQF level 2) and 697 (millwright, NQF level 4). All programmes have a knowledge, practical skills and work experience module.

Skills programmes

The Skills Development Act describes skills programmes as unit standard-based programmes that are occupationally based and delivered by an accredited training provider, and when completed, constitute credits towards a qualification registered in terms of the NQF. A skills programme can be considered a mini-qualification in that it comprises an agreed unit standard or cluster of unit standards. The registration of skills programmes is the responsibility of the SETAs.

Source: Human Resource Development Council for South Africa (2014[24]); Department for Higher Education and Training (2016[22]).

Part-qualifications, like the skills programmes offered by SETAs, could be the best option for CET. These skills programmes are a combination of one or more unit standards and provide NQF credits (but not full NQF qualifications) (see Box 3.3). These short-term skills programmes would allow individuals to acquire relatively quickly the skills that are in demand in their local labour market, such that they can easily progress into work. For those individuals who would like to continue into further education and training, the part-qualifications give them a first basis on which they can build further.

Skills programmes already offered in Community Learning Centres have mainly been targeted at traditional trades, but this does not necessarily have to be the case. In France, subsidized training programmes are available for disadvantaged youth to develop specialised IT skills (see Box 3.4). Some NGOs, employers or training providers might already be offering skills training programmes that respond to the needs of the community. It could be an option to form partnerships with these providers and allocate subsidies for continuing or expanding their training programme if needed. This type of set-up would avoid duplication of investment and would allow making optimal use of the already available knowledge, expertise and equipment. It should be noted that setting up and managing partnerships also requires sufficient dedicated resources and capacity, as partnerships generally involve extensive administration, but also additional quality assurance and monitoring mechanisms.

Box 3.4. Equipping disadvantaged youth with specialised IT skills in France

The French Government introduced the *Grande École du Numérique* label in 2015, granting labels of excellence to short-term (1 to 42 months) IT training courses that respond to specific labour market needs, such as coding or web development. The needs should be identified in co-operation with regional and professional stakeholders, and training should involve soft skills that are valued by employers. Subsidies are available for training providers that get their training labelled. The *Grande École du Numérique* courses are subsidised (fully or partially), and open to everyone irrespective of academic background. While open to everyone, the training focusses on low-skilled youth, setting a target of 50% low-skilled NEETs among participants. Efforts are also done to attract female students (with a target of 30%) and students from disadvantaged areas. By mid-2018, 410 trainings programmes received the *Grande École du Numérique* label, and over 11 000 students participated. The average duration of training programmes equals around seven months.

The latest information on the participants in *Grande École du Numérique* programmes shows that the initiative has been able to reach its target audience: 65% of students are NEET, 55% have at most upper secondary education, 24% are women and 17% come from disadvantaged areas. The professional pathways of graduates show a relatively positive picture: 74% of graduates are employed or in further education or training.

Source: OECD (2017[25]); Grande école du numérique (2018[26]).

Students and graduates from these skills programmes would benefit from additional on-the-job learning during their studies or immediately after graduation. Internships provide a good opportunity for individuals to further develop their skills on the job, and for employers to "test out" potential new recruits. Employers can get funding for internships from SETAs through the skills development levy system. At the same time, participants in skills programmes could also be encouraged to participate in non-formal programmes to reinforce their employability skills (see Section 3.4), which could facilitate their transition into the labour market. The *+Capaz* programme in Chile integrates transversal skills training in vocational programmes, and provides the opportunity to participants to also take part in practical training (see Box 3.5).

Recommended action steps

Table 3.4 provides some possible action steps that could be taken to implement and improve vocational skills programmes in CET. For each action step, the most relevant stakeholders concerned are listed. The list of stakeholders is not exhaustive, and cooperation between different stakeholders is encouraged. The actions steps focus on the short- and medium-term, and a more ambitious action plan could be developed for the longer term in line with the vision for CET from the DHET's strategic documents.

Table 3.4. Actions steps for vocational skills programmes

Action steps and relevant stakeholders

Action steps	Main stakeholders
Take stock of the already available vocational skills training programmes and training facilities in the local communities	All
Decide on which training programmes to offer at CET institutions and which external providers to enter into partnerships with, in accordance with community needs (see Chapter 5)	CET Colleges, CLCs
Develop new vocational skills programmes (when needed) in close cooperation with SETAs and local employers (see Chapter 5)	CLCs, SETAs, employers
Make sure that accreditation of skills programmes (by SETAs and the relevant quality council) happens thoroughly, but swiftly. For SETAs who have limited experience or a poor track record in registering skills programmes, training and guidelines should be offered.	SETAs, DHET, SAQA, Quality Councils
Engage with local employers and SETAs to make sure that internship opportunities are available for CET graduates (see Chapter 5)	CLCs, SETAs, employers
Ensure that accompanying soft skills and remedial programmes are also available for vocational skills students, in order for them to increase their employability. Promote these programmes actively among the vocational skills students.	CLCs
Increase the flexibility of programmes in TVET colleges (e.g. part-time and distance provision), so that adults with the motivation and capacities to enter the TVET system also have easy access.	DHET, TVET colleges
Coordinate closely with TVET colleges in the region to ensure that there are easy pathways from the CET vocational skills programmes into TVET programmes.	CET Colleges, CLCs, TVET colleges, SAQA, Quality Councils

Note: DHET: Department for Higher Education and Training; CLC: Community Learning Centre; SETA: Sector Education and Training Authority; TVET: Technical and Vocational Education and Training; SAQA: South African Qualifications Authority; NGO: Non-Governmental Organisation.

Box 3.5. +Capaz: Occupational skills training for vulnerable groups in Chile

The +Capaz programme was introduced in Chile in 2015, offering subsidised training to vulnerable youth and women, as well as disabled persons. The programme is only open to the population with low levels of income and with no or weak labour market attachment. The +Capaz programme is composed of:

- *Learning phase*: Participants take part in training programmes in trades with a duration of between 180 and 300 hours. The Public Employment Service (PES) selects the programmes based on labour market needs. Each programme, irrespective of the trade, includes a 60-hour transversal skills package. The programmes are delivered by Technical training organisations, TVET colleges, higher education institutions and NGOs, which receive payments for every hour of training provided under the +Capaz programme. A minimum attendance of 75% is required to successfully finish the learning phase.

- *Employment intermediation*: Participants who have completed the learning phase can benefit from employment intermediation, consisting of (optional) practical training and job placement. Employment intermediation is the responsibility of the training providers, which receive payments for each job placements with a minimum employment duration of three months and a salary at least equal to the minimum wage.
- *Education level upgrading*: Participants who did not finish secondary education can participate in a 150-hours training programme to prepare for the national examinations.
- *Continuing education*: Participants with upper secondary educational attainment who finished the +Capaz programme can receive financing to continue their education in the same field as the +Capaz training. The +Capaz training is recognized as an initial module in higher education.
- *Recognition*: Around 20% of participants who finish the learning phase can get their previous work experience recognized through the Chilean system for Recognition of Prior Learning.

Participants receive transport and food allowances, as well as accident insurance. Participants with children younger than six years old can benefit from childcare. In recognition of the fact that skills gaps are not the only barrier to labour market participation for the +Capaz target group, personalised socio-labour support, including career guidance, is provided to participants during the learning phase.

The programme was piloted in 2014 with around 3000 participants. The goal of the programme is to train 450 000 individuals in the period 2014-18. An evaluation of the first year of the programme showed that 5% of participants dropped out during the programme, and an additional 17% had to re-take the programme because of low attendance. A preliminary analysis of labour market outcomes of 2015 participants showed that 11.4% of participants found work within three months after completion of the learning phase and stayed in work for at least three months. The share increases to 24.3% when looking at at least one month of employment in the three months following the completion of the learning phase.[1] The labour market outcomes are better for male youth (42.9%, using the one month employment requirement) than for female youth (27.1%) and female adults (17.4%). Looking at the evolution of employment rates of participants after finishing the programme, the analysis shows an average monthly increase of the rate of 2.4 percentage points.

A second evaluation exercise in 2016 showed that the program had positive, albeit small, and consistent impacts on labour market participation, duration of employment and wages of participants. The evaluation highlighted the importance of personalised support and the availability of childcare. Some weaknesses of the programme were also brought to light, including the fact that the practical training, while useful, was not an attractive option for participants because it delayed access to paid employment and childcare was not available. Another important weakness of the programme was the lack of experience of training providers in employment intermediation, resulting in low placement rates.

Source: Brown et al. (2016[27]); ClioDinámica Asesorías (2017[28])

3.4. Non-formal programmes

The South African skills system is very strongly focused on formal training, registered on the NQF. Under the levy system, for example, the PIVOTAL requirement that 80% of the discretionary grants is earmarked for training on scarce and critical skills (see Chapter 1) limits eligible training to quality assured training registered on the NQF. While the formal training system clearly has the advantage of an established quality assurance system, it is relatively rigid. Many training programmes that are useful from an employer and employee or job-seeker perspective do not fit into the NQF. To complement the formal programmes, CET should also provide useful non-formal training opportunities. As for skills programmes, non-formal programmes might already be delivered by non-government providers, and these providers could potentially be subsided to continue or expand their offer. The CET system could provide non-formal training programmes in a variety of areas:

Employability skills: These training programmes should help participants, and especially those with limited work experience, in finding suitable job opportunities and adjusting more easily to the workplace environment. Employability skills include, for example, CV-writing, job interview training, but also softer skills training such as punctuality, politeness and familiarity with workplace practises. The curricula for employability skills programmes could be based on existing guides describing skill required in the workplace, as many employers have some type of workplace readiness programmes (see Box 3.6).

Box 3.6. Employers' workplace readiness programmes

New hires often lack the soft skills that are needed in the workplace. This is especially the case for youth and adults with no or limited work experience. Employers sometimes help their new hires develop these critical skills through short workplace readiness programmes.

EOH, a large technology service provider in South Africa, organises workshops for their newly hired employees with the purpose of developing critical interpersonal skills, work ethic and understanding of the dynamics of a workplace. Their programme consists of five modules: i) Big picture thinking, ii) Interpersonal awareness, iii) Structured thinking, iv) Analytical thinking, and v) Innovation and creative thinking. Topics covered in the EOH workplace readiness programme include working within a team, professional dress code, communicating effectively, handling feedback appropriately, and managing time. The programme is described in detailed in an accompanying learner guide.

Source: EOH Learning & Development (2016[29])

Entrepreneurship and management skills: These programmes could be delivered to help individuals set up their own business. This includes training on practical things such as how to develop a business plan or obtain funding, but also training in areas such as accounting. Survey evidence suggests that only 38% of South African adults believe they have the skills and knowledge to start a business, which is much lower than in many other emerging economies (see Figure 3.1). CET institutions that deliver these programmes should have close ties with employers in their community, so that new start-ups can have a network of mentors that can give them practical advice. Individuals who are already operating an informal business should be able to participate in these types of programmes to help them formalise their business.

Figure 3.1. Perceived entrepreneurial capabilities are low in South Africa

Share of population (aged 18-64) who believe to have the required skills and knowledge to start a business (2014)

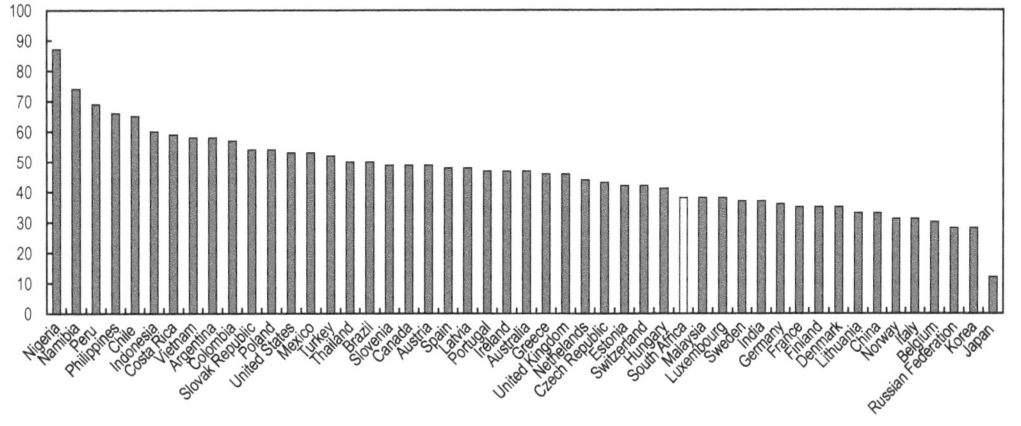

Note: 2013 data for Czech Republic, Latvia, Namibia, Nigeria, Korea and Turkey.
Source: Global Entrepreneurship Monitor.

Digital skills: Possessing the skills needed to use digital tools and technologies is becoming increasingly important, not only in the labour market but also in daily life. Digital skills programmes could teach participants the basics of computer use, including the use of word processing and spreadsheets, but also how to search the internet and use social media. In Mexico, adults can participate in digital skills programmes in digital inclusion centres spread across the country (see Box 3.7). In addition, more specialised digital programmes could be offered, such as programming or coding (as in the example of France discussed above in Box 3.4). Multiple organisations in South Africa are specialised in organising these types of digital programmes for youth and adults. WeThinkCode, for example, offers a tuition-free two-year coding programme that is sponsored by companies and is open and accessible to all talented young people (17-35 years old), irrespective of their educational background.

Life skills: Communities would also benefit from non-formal training in areas such as healthcare, wellbeing, climate change and anti-corruption. This can take the form of seminars and workshops, but also short-term training programmes. Other actors might already be delivering these types of life skills programmes, including NGOs and other government Departments.

Several countries have set up training institutions that provide both formal and non-formal training. In Argentina, a new type of intuition, the *Casas del Futuro*, was introduced in 2016, bringing together vocational skills and non-formal programmes (see Box 3.8). Sweden and other Scandinavian countries have a long tradition of Folk high schools, which provide second change education, non-formal training and vocational skill programmes (see Box 3.9).

Box 3.7. Digital inclusion centres in Mexico

In Mexico, a national network of community learning centres focussing on digital skills education and training was established in 2015. The network currently consists of 32 centres (*Puntos Mexico Conectado*), spread over the different states. These centres are open to everyone and provide access to digital technologies and training on how to use them. Training is available in four areas:

- Digital ABC: These courses help individuals develop basic digital skills for day-to-day use, including browsing the internet and using a computer for personal finances.
- Miscellaneous digital programmes: In these programmes, children and adults use digital technologies in a practical and entertaining way to stimulate curiosity and creativity. Examples include robotics and programming courses.
- Digital innovation and entrepreneurship: This programme helps aspiring entrepreneurs to develop new products and business plans, and existing entrepreneurs to improve their performance. The programme consists of three phases: design, create and implement.
- Digital culture: Open space where people can discover the talent of new artists in the digital world. The aim is to promote the use of technology in daily lives.

Three years after its inception, the network of community learning centres counts 636 000 registered members and 465 000 individuals participate in the programmes.

Source: Gobierno de la Republica (2018[30]); Secretaría de Comunicaciones y Transportes (2018[31])

Recommended action steps

Table 3.5 provides some possible action steps that could be taken to implement and improve non-formal programmes in CET. For each action step, the most relevant stakeholders concerned are listed. The list of stakeholders is not exhaustive, and cooperation between different stakeholders is encouraged. The actions focus on the short- and medium-term, and a more ambitious action plan could be developed for the longer term in line with the vision for CET from the DHET's strategic documents.

Table 3.5. Action steps for non-formal programmes

Action steps and relevant stakeholders

Action steps	Main stakeholders
Decide on which non-formal programmes to offer and their content in close cooperation with local NGOs, employers and government departments (see Chapter 5)	CET Colleges, CLC, NGOs, employers, DHET and other government departments
Develop a close network of formal and informal SMMEs that could serves as mentors for students from the entrepreneurship skills programme	CLCs
Develop standardized CET certificates that serve as proof of (successful) completion of some of the non-formal programmes	DHET

Note: DHET: Department for Higher Education and Training; CLC: Community Learning Centre; NGO: Non-Governmental Organisation.

Box 3.8. *Casas del Futuro* – Offering training and guidance for Argentinian youth

The first *Casa del Futuro* was opened in Argentina in 2016, with the aim to provide opportunities for personal development to youth aged 15 to 24. Currently, three *Casas del Futuro* are operational in Argentina, located in areas with a large group of vulnerable youth. The project provides free workshops, training in traditional and digital trades, cultural activities and sports. Courses include digital literacy, robotics, new technologies, coding, languages, journalism, but also yoga, dance and painting. Talks are organised on topics such as sexuality, violence and addictions. The project also provides career guidance and information on government programmes. The project is led by an interdisciplinary team, which stimulates, supports and follows up the participants.

The *Casas del Futuro* have strong links with organisations, industries and firms in their communities, as such creating a network that facilitates the entry of participants into the labour market. Course offerings, especially for the traditional trades, are determined in line with community needs. Between 2016 and mid-2018, almost 11 000 youth visited the centres, and over 1 300 activities were organised. The majority of participants are over 18 years old, and there are more female than male participants. Many of the participants are also enrolled in formal education institutions, be it at the secondary level or higher.

In recognition of the work that non-governmental organisations are doing to help vulnerable youth, the Argentinian government put in place the *Acá Estamos* programme. The aim of the programme is to develop closer ties with these non-governmental organisations and to reinforce them to become key spaces for vulnerable youth to work on personal development. In the second phase of the *Acá Estamos* programme, the government wants to further develop the relationships with these organisations and help them grow, by providing equipment and training. Over time, some of these projects could become similar to *Casas del Futuro*, with the benefit that they require less infrastructure investment than the traditional *Casas de Futuro* (which need to be built from scratch).

Source: Ministerio de Desarrollo Social (2016[32])

3.5. Information, guidance and recognition of prior learning

Giving information and guidance to adults about different training options

Adults need to have information about their different education and training options. Learners who choose programmes that meet their interest and preferences, and for which they have clear expectations, are more likely to be successful in such programmes and complete them (Musset and Mytna Kurekova, 2018[7]). A first step to better inform adults about the CET system and the programmes it offers, could be to launch a comprehensive communication campaign together with an exhaustive website. The emphasis of such an information campaign should be on the value of acquiring skills in adulthood, and the range of programmes available and their labour market outcomes. An interesting example of a website with comprehensive information on training programmes can be found in Peru, where the Ministries of Education and Labour's website "*Ponte en Carrera*" (Get into a career) provides data on the cost and labour market outcomes of specific programmes of study at all of the country's technical institutes and universities (McCarthy and Musset, 2016[33]).

Box 3.9. Folk high schools: Providing second chance and non-formal training in Sweden

Folk high schools in Sweden are independent adult education institutions that provide a range of education and training programmes. The concept of Folk high school was introduced in Sweden in 1868, and today around 150 schools are operational across the country. Swedish folk high schools offer:

- *Second chance education*: Students can participate in a General Courses programme that allows them to catch up to an upper secondary level and get access to higher education
- *Non-formal programmes*: Non-formal programmes are mainly offered in the field of arts, health, environment and nature, international topics and languages, media and communication, and society and religion.
- *Vocational programmes:* Vocational programmes are offered at the upper-secondary and the post-secondary level. Examples of vocational programmes include journalism, personal assistant and treatment assistant.

Around two-thirds of folk high schools are run by popular movements in civic society, such as organisations within the workers' temperance or Free Church movements, while the rest are run by county councils or regions. Folk High Schools are not bound by national curricula: each folk high school decides independently what courses it provides, and freely designs its teaching. Many Folk high school offer boarding for students.

In addition to Folk high schools, Sweden also has a system of study associations that organise study circles across the country. Jointly, the folk high schools and study associations are known as *Folkbildning*. The main priorities of the system are: i) enlightenment and context, ii) accessibility and inclusion, iii) citizens and civil society, iv) working life and lifelong learning, and v) culture and creativity.

Every year, Folk high schools welcome around 90 000 participants in short courses and 27 000 in long courses. The biggest group of participants are youth aged 18-24. The majority of participants in long courses have low levels of education attainment. A survey among 2013 Folk high school students showed that they are largely satisfied, as their studies gave them better opportunities for continuing education and training and in the labour market. Participants also reported that the Folk high school studies stimulated their interest in social issues and culture, and helped bolster their self-confidence. Satisfaction is highest among women and foreign-born.

Source: OECD (2016[34]); Folkbildningsrådet (2013[35]; 2015[36]).

Given that only a limited number of programmes will be provided in each Community Learning Centre, it is important that individuals understand which training options exist in their community or close by. CET counsellors should inform individuals about the programmes available in Community Learning Centres, and provide information on: further education programmes in the colleges and universities in the region, and about the financial support available; NGO training programmes; and training programmes provided or funded, for example, by SETAs, employers or the Unemployment Insurance Fund. The counsellors should actively promote training that is relevant to community needs. This approach should be taken together with the development of specific information sources to adults outside and independently of the institutions themselves.

At the same time, the CET counsellors should also provide guidance on labour market opportunities. For this they should cooperate with the South African Public Employment Service (Employment Service South Africa, ESSA), but also be in close contact with the employers in the community, both in the formal and informal sector. Good career guidance services provide job seekers with a wide range of resources, as is the case for the career guidance providers in the *Cité des Métiers* network (see Box 3.10).

The Department for Higher Education and Training offers elaborate career development services (Kheta), including a career advice helpline, radio programmes that provide information and advice on careers, and a website that helps individuals make informed education, training and career choices (National Career Advice Portal). These existing resources and services should be used as much as possible to provide guidance and information in CET institutions.

Box 3.10. *Cité des Métiers* – A worldwide network of career guidance providers

A *Cité des Métiers* is a place where people can find information on how to build their professional future. Cités are built on the principles of open access and free of charge and anonymous use. The mission of the *Cités des Métiers* is to give users access to resources that should help them formulate and achieve their career goals and support them in their choices. This is done by providing in one single space:

- Interviews with professionals from the fields of counselling and professional life
- Free access documentation on employment, careers and vocational training
- IT resources and multimedia areas
- One-day information sessions, symposia and meetings organised by the Cité's partners or produced in cooperation with external partners

These services are provided in five areas: i) choose your career path, ii) find a job, iii) change your professional life, evolve, validate your skills and experience, iv) organise your career path and training, and v) create your own business. The services are open to everyone, irrespective of age and labour market status.

Institutions can submit a request to obtain the *Cité des Métiers* label. The first Cité was opened in France in 1993, and today they can be found in nine countries: Belgium, Canada, France, Germany, Italy, Portugal, Spain, Switzerland and Togo. Within the common framework, each individual Cité can develop its own activities based on the needs of its target audience.

Source: Cité des Sciences et de l'Industrie (2018[37]).

Recognising existing skills to give more flexibility

Recognition of prior learning (RPL) is an important tool to help individuals find employment opportunities or advance in their career, especially in a country like South Africa where many people have been denied access to formal education and training in the past. In practice, many adults have work experience and/or acquired skills both formally and informally. Skill recognition can reduce the direct and opportunity costs of formal learning. It can helps motivating adults and sustain their engagement in education and training programmes (Kis and Windisch, 2018[38]).

All qualifications registered on the National Qualifications Framework can be obtained in whole or part through RPL. OECD (2017[39]) points out that, while the RPL system is well developed in South Africa, there are multiple barriers for people to use it, including lack of awareness and complexity. CET could play a role in making better use of existing RPL opportunities, by providing guidance and assistance. CET Counsellors can help promote RPL in communities, and identify people who could benefit from it. Additionally, CET staff could assist RPL candidates in putting together their portfolio. The use of RPL to shorten programme duration and potentially increase completion would require developing the skills of staff in CET institutions so that they are capable of RPL assessments, acknowledging that these procedures can be costly and time-consuming. Breaking down education and training programmes into discrete modules to allow for course exemptions and different paces of study can also be challenging (OECD, 2014[40]).

Recommended action steps

Table 3.6 provides some possible action steps that could be taken to provide information, guidance and RPL services in CET. For each action step, the most relevant stakeholders concerned are listed. The list of stakeholders is not exhaustive, and cooperation between different stakeholders is encouraged. The actions steps focus on the short- and medium-term, and a more ambitious action plan could be developed for the longer term in line with the vision for CET from the DHET's strategic documents.

Table 3.6. Actions steps for information, guidance and RPL

Action steps and relevant stakeholders

Action steps	Main stakeholders
Improve information about CET provision and launch a comprehensive communication campaign to raise awareness of the CET system and the new skills programmes it offers	DHET, CET Colleges, ESSA
Meet with training providers in the region to understand their course offering. Ask for brochures on their programmes to make available at CET institutions.	CET Colleges, CLCs, TVET colleges, universities, private providers, NGOs
Develop materials on government support for further education and training to be made available at CET institutions (e.g. NSFAS bursaries).	DHET
Facilitate coordination between CET institutions and Labour Centres. CET counsellors should have up-to-date knowledge of job vacancies at Labour Centres and should refer individuals to register with the Labour Centres, and Labour Centre workers should have a good understanding of the courses and services offered at the CET institutions. (see Chapter 5)	CET Colleges, CLCs, Labour Centres, DHET, DoL
Train CET staff to be able to deliver guidance in terms of training and job opportunities. Counsellors should keep their knowledge up-to-date through regular training, especially concerning available training opportunities and labour market needs.	DHET, CET Colleges, CLCs
Train CET staff to better understand the functioning and requirements of RPL, so they can offer guidance and assistance to interested individuals. This training can be done by experienced staff from TVET colleges and universities	DHET, CET Colleges, CLCs, TVET colleges, universities, SAQA
Develop materials that can be used by CET staff to assist individuals in the elaboration of their RPL portfolio. Organise information sessions on RPL, possibly in cooperation with nearby TVET colleges	DHET, CET Colleges, CLCs, SAQA,TVET colleges

Note: DHET: Department for Higher Education and Training; DoL: Department of Labour; CLC: Community Learning Centre; TVET: Technical and Vocational Education and Training; SAQA: South African Qualifications Authority; NGO: Non-Governmental Organisation.

Note

[1] The Chilean labour market is characterised by a large share of (short) temporary contracts. The share of temporary workers (as a percentage of dependant workers) is the highest among OECD countries (28% in 2017, compared to the OECD average of 11%). Just over 45% of dependent workers in Chile have tenure below six months (the OECD average is 31%). (OECD Labour Force Statistics Database)

References

Autorengruppe Bildungsberichterstattung (2018), *Bildung in Deutschland 2018: Ein indikatorengesützter Bericht mit einer Analyse zu Wirkungen und Erträgen von Bildung*, http://dx.doi.org/10.3278/6001820fw. [17]

Avramovska, M., E. Hirsch and B. Schmidt-Behlau (2017), "Adult education centres as a key to development – challenges and success factors", *International Perspectives in Adult Education*, No. 78, DVV International, Bonn. [13]

Beicht, U. (2009), "Verbesserung der Ausbildungs-chancen oder sinnlose Warteschleife?", *BIBB Report*, No. 11/09, BIBB, Bonn. [18]

Brown, C. et al. (2016), *Primer año del Programa +Capaz: Evidencia sobre insercion laboral de egresados*, Ministerio del Trabajo y Previson Social. [27]

Bynner, J. and S. Parsons (2006), *New Light on Literacy and Numeracy*, National Research and Development Centre for Adult Literacy and Numeracy (NDRC), http://www.nrdc.org.uk/publications_details.asp?ID=78. [15]

Cité des Sciences et de l'Industrie (2018), *Cité des métiers - Information et conseil sans rendez-vous*, http://www.cite-sciences.fr/fr/au-programme/lieux-ressources/cite-des-metiers/ (accessed on 30 April 2018). [37]

ClioDinámica Asesorías (2017), *Evaluacion de implementacion y resultados programa Mas Capaz año 2016*, Servicio Nacional de Capacitacion y Empleo. [28]

Department of Higher Education and Training (2016), *Statistics on Post-School Education and Training in South Africa Statistics on Post-School Education and Training in South Africaa*, Department for Higher Education and Training. [22]

Desjardins, R. (2017), *Political economy of adult learning systems: Comparative study of strategies, policies and constraints*, Bloomsbury, London, https://www.bloomsbury.com/uk/political-economy-of-adult-learning-systems-9781474273664/ (accessed on 13 September 2018). [1]

Direction de la Lutte Contre l'Analphabétisme (2012), *Alphabétisation au Maroc: Plan d'action 2012-2015*, Ministère de l'Education Nationale, http://www.unesco.org/new/fileadmin/MULTIMEDIA/HQ/ED/pdf/Maroc.pdf (accessed on 12 June 2018). [11]

Eichhorst, W., F. Wozny and M. Cox (2015), "Policy Performance and Evaluation: Germany", *IZA Research Report* 66, http://legacy.iza.org/en/webcontent/publications/reports/report_pdfs/iza_report_66.pdf (accessed on 31 May 2018). [19]

EOH Learning & Development (2016), *The EOH Workplace Readiness Programme - Learner guide*, EOH. [29]

Erban, T. (2010), *Das Berufsvorbereitungsjahr als Übergang von der Schule zum Beruf : eine Längsschnittuntersuchung zum Verbleib eines Absolventenjahrgangs und zur Wirksamkeit des Berufsvorbereitungsjahres*, Peter Lang. [20]

Fialho, P., G. Quintini and M. Vandeweyer (2019), "Returns to different forms of job-related training: Factoring in informal learning", *OECD Social Employment and Migration working paper*, forthcoming. [2]

Field, S., P. Musset and J. Álvarez-Galván (2014), *A Skills beyond School Review of South Africa*, OECD Reviews of Vocational Education and Training, OECD Publishing, Paris, http://dx.doi.org/10.1787/9789264223776-en. [23]

Folkbildningsrådet (2015), *Steget vidare – undersökning bland folkhögskolans deltagare 2013*, https://issuu.com/folkbildningsradet/docs/fbr_rapport_utvardering_1_2015_webb/1?ff=true&e=7205506/30646064 (accessed on 27 April 2018). [36]

Folkbildningsrådet (2013), *Folkbildning's Direction & Intent: On the role and tasks of Swedish study associations and Folk high schools in current and future society*, https://issuu.com/folkbildningsradet/docs/direction-intent/1?ff=true&e=7205506/6053894 (accessed on 27 April 2018). [35]

Gobierno de la Republica (2018), *Punto México Conectado - Centro de inclusion digital*, http://www.pmc.gob.mx/ (accessed on 10 July 2018). [30]

Grande école du numérique (2018), *Grande école du numérique: Chiffres clés 2017*, Grande école du numérique, Paris, https://www.grandeecolenumerique.fr/wp-content/uploads/2018/06/ChiffresCles2017_GEN_WEBVF.pdf (accessed on 10 July 2018). [26]

Human Resource Development Council for South Africa (2014), *TVET Colleges in South Africa: Pathways Workstream*, http://hrdcsa.org.za/wp-content/uploads/research-reports/PATHWAYS%20-%20TVETColleges%20in%20South%20Africa%20REPORT%20-%2015%20August.pdf (accessed on 3 May 2018). [24]

Kis, V. and H. Windisch (2018), "Making skills transparent: Recognising vocational skills acquired through workbased learning", *OECD Education Working Papers*, No. 180, OECD, Paris, https://www.oecd-ilibrary.org/education/making-skills-transparent_5830c400-en (accessed on 4 February 2019). [38]

Kuczera, M. and S. Field (2013), *A Skills beyond School Review of the United States*, OECD Reviews of Vocational Education and Training, OECD Publishing, Paris, http://dx.doi.org/10.1787/9789264202153-en. [16]

Kuczera, M., S. Field and H. Windisch (2015), *Building Skills for All: a Review of England. Policy Insights from the Survey of Adult Skills*, OECD Skills Studies OECD Publishing, https://www.oecd.org/unitedkingdom/building-skills-for-all-review-of-england.pdf. [14]

Lolwana, P., E. Rabe and M. Morakane (2018), "Who accesses adult education and where do they progress to? An exploratory tracer study in community education and training", *LMIP reports*, No. 37, Labour Market Intelligence Parternship, http://www.lmip.org.za/document/who-accesses-adult-education-and-where-do-they-progress-exploratory-tracer-study-community (accessed on 7 November 2018). [10]

McCarthy, M. and P. Musset (2016), *A Skills beyond School Review of Peru*, OECD Reviews of Vocational Education and Training, OECD Publishing, Paris, http://dx.doi.org/10.1787/9789264265400-en. [33]

Ministerio de Desarrollo Social (2016), *Los jóvenes tendrán su lugar de encuentro con la Casa del Futuro*, http://www.desarrollosocial.gob.ar/noticias/casa-futuro (accessed on 30 April 2018). [32]

Musset, P. (2015), *Building Skills For All: A Review of Finland. Policy Insights on Literacy, Numeracy and Digital Skills from the Survey of Adult Skills*, OECD Publishing, http://www.oecd.org/finland/Building-Skills-For-All-A-Review-of-Finland.pdf. [5]

Musset, P. and L. Mytna Kurekova (2018), "Working it out: Career Guidance and Employer Engagement", *OECD Education Working Papers*, No. 175, OECD Publishing, Paris, http://dx.doi.org/10.1787/51c9d18d-en. [7]

OECD (2019), *Getting Skills Right: Future-Ready Adult Learning Systems*, Getting Skills Right, OECD Publishing, Paris, https://dx.doi.org/10.1787/9789264311756-en. [4]

OECD (2017), *Education at a Glance 2017: OECD Indicators*, OECD Publishing, Paris, http://dx.doi.org/10.1787/eag-2017-en. [3]

OECD (2017), *Getting Skills Right: France*, Getting Skills Right, OECD Publishing, Paris, http://dx.doi.org/10.1787/9789264284456-en. [25]

OECD (2017), *Getting Skills Right: South Africa*, Getting Skills Right, OECD Publishing, Paris, http://dx.doi.org/10.1787/9789264278745-en. [39]

OECD (2016), *Investing in Youth: Sweden*, OECD Publishing, Paris, http://dx.doi.org/10.1787/9789264267701-en. [34]

OECD (2014), *Skills beyond School: Synthesis Report*, OECD Reviews of Vocational Education and Training, OECD Publishing, Paris, http://dx.doi.org/10.1787/9789264214682-en. [40]

OECD (2010), *Learning for Jobs*, OECD Reviews of Vocational Education and Training, OECD Publishing, Paris, http://dx.doi.org/10.1787/9789264087460-en. [8]

Secretaría de Comunicaciones y Transportes (2018), "Reforma de Telecomunicaciones suma a 40 millones de nuevos usuarios de internet", *Comunicado-336-2018*, https://www.gob.mx/sct/prensa/reforma-de-telecomunicaciones-suma-a-40-millones-de-nuevos-usuarios-de-internet (accessed on 8 November 2018). [31]

Statistisches Bundesamt (2018), "Berufliche Schulen - Schuljahr 2016/2017", *Bildung und Kultur*, No. 11/2, Statistisches Bundesamt. [21]

Unesco (2012), *Community learning centres: Asia-Pacific regional conference report*, Unesco Asia and Pacific Regional Bureau for Education, Bangkok, http://unesdoc.unesco.org/images/0021/002159/215911e.pdf (accessed on 6 August 2018). [9]

UNESCO Institute for Lifelong Learning (2013), *Literacy Programmes with a focus on women to reduce gender disparities*, http://www.unesco.org/uil/litbase/ (accessed on 12 June 2018). [12]

Windisch, H. (2015), "Adults with low literacy and numeracy skills: A literature review on policy intervention", *OECD Education Working Papers*, No. 123, OECD Publishing, Paris, http://dx.doi.org/10.1787/5jrxnjdd3r5k-en. [6]

Chapter 4. Financing Community Education and Training

The improvement and further development of South Africa's community education and training system will require considerable investment. This investment is needed to further improve current provision, but also to pilot and roll out new training programmes and services. This chapter looks at possible sources of funding for the community education and training system, and highlights the priority funding areas for which these resources should be mobilised.

4.1. Background

In most countries, the resources allocated to training opportunities for adults are much smaller than those for compulsory and post-secondary education. According to FiBS and DIE (2013[1]), total adult learning spending (by all actors) across a set of OECD countries in 2009 accounted for 0.9% of GDP on average, compared to 2.7% of GDP for primary education, 1.3% for upper secondary education, and 1.6% for tertiary education. The main contributors to the financing of adult education and training are generally employers, individuals and governments. The share of these actors in total spending varies between countries, but on average across OECD countries with available information, employers bear the largest share of adult learning costs (45% of total spending on adult learning on average), followed by individuals (23.3%) and the state (21%) (FiBS and DIE, 2013[1]). In general, comprehensive and comparable data on expenditure on adult learning is scant, mainly because of the scattered nature of the adult learning policy domain that has many different stakeholders involved in the financing and delivery of training programmes.

As argued by OECD (2019[2]), it would be advisable to have a health mix of financial resources for adult education and training, as benefits of a better skilled population accrue to employers, individuals and the society more broadly. Governments contribute to this healthy mix by directly providing fully subsidized training opportunities, but also indirectly through the availability of financial incentives, such as subsidies and tax deductions.

In general, financing of education and training can be analysed from three perspectives (UNESCO, 2017[3]):

- *Adequacy*: Ensuring that sufficient resources are mobilised to provide education and training of high quality for all participants. Without reaching a minimum threshold of inputs and resources, the education and training system cannot produce the expected results. To ensure adequacy of the budget, many countries do not rely on public funding only, but also attract private resources.
- *Efficiency: M*obilising and managing financial resources to provide good quality and effective education services at the least cost. In decentralised systems, efficient allocation of funds to schools ensures that resources available for schools correspond to their specific needs and performance (e.g. in terms of student numbers, share of disadvantaged students, learning outcomes). An efficient use of funding also means avoiding duplication of investment.
- *Equity*: Resources need to be allocated in an equitable way that is both fair and conductive to inclusiveness. In order to address equity concerns it is necessary to adjust spending to reach disadvantaged groups. Resource allocation to schools needs to take into account the particular challenges involved in reaching disadvantaged groups and ensuring high completion rate for these groups.

All three elements are crucial and well-functioning education and training systems take a holistic approach to financing that ensures adequacy, efficiency and equity at the same time. As pointed out by OECD (2017[4]), the sources of education funding are becoming increasingly diverse. While the central government remains the main funder of education institutions in most countries, other actors, such as sub-central governments and private actors, are increasingly providing complementary funds. In such a multi-level and multi-actor governance system of funding, adequate institutional and regulatory frameworks to optimise the role of each actor in ensuring an effective and equitable allocation of funds becomes crucial.

4.2. Potential funding sources

Public funding for CET is limited today (see Chapter 1), and it will be crucial to attract additional funding to achieve the desired growth to reach the target of 1 million adult participants by 2030. A projection exercise calculated that if funding for CET were to follow its historical trend, there would be a ZAR 16.88 billion shortfall to reach the White Paper's goals by 2030 (DNA Economics, 2016[5]).[1] While this exercise is based on a set of strong assumptions, it does provide a useful ballpark estimate of required additional funding. In ensuring that sufficient funding is available for the expansion and improvement of CET in South Africa, a mix of financial resources should be attracted, avoiding too much of the burden falling on one actor. Resources could be mobilised from different government departments, employers, individuals and external donors. Several policy documents related to CET have explicitly mentioned that the financial burden on individuals should be minimised, especially since the target audience of CET consists largely of disadvantaged adults with limited financial resources.

Different levels of government contribute to the financing of training opportunities

As discussed in Chapter 1, national government expenditure on CET is relatively low, and is not expected to increase substantially in the short or medium term. Especially in light of the relatively modest growth forecasts for the South African economy[2], the budgetary situation will probably remain tight in the coming years. For the financial year 2017/18, the budget for CET equals ZAR 2 198 million. This central government budget is almost entirely reserved for expenditure on compensation of employees (92.3%), leaving only a very small amount for the investment in further development of the CET system. While it is highly unlikely that the CET system will be granted a large amount of extra funding from the National Treasury in the coming years, the Department for Higher Education and Training could request additional funding for specific areas or pilot projects. For this, it will be important for the Department to have clear and well-developed plans.

Provincial governments also invest in skills development, albeit generally outside the CET system. Receipts in the provincial budget mainly consist of transfers from the national government. To get a sense of the size of the provincial budgets, the estimated 2017/18 total budget for the Gauteng province, which accounts for 25.3% of the South African population, equals ZAR 108.8 billion. The largest shares of the provincial budgets are spent on (basic) education and health (37.6% and 37.0% respectively in the Gauteng Province). Skills development outside of basic education can be part of different areas of provincial budgets. In the Gauteng province, for example, the budget sets targets for youth skills development (37 651 participants), parenting skills programmes (15 531 families) and skills development and training programmes for integrated economic development (2 685 participants). Box 4.1 provides an example of a large-scale skills programme led by the Gauteng province.

Municipal governments also have their own budget to invest in a range of areas. Part of their budget comes from national and provincial government transfers, but the majority are own revenues, like property rates and the sale of electricity and water. The largest expenditure areas are employee-related costs and the purchase of electricity (Statistics South Africa, 2017[6]). One of the objectives of municipalities is to promote social and economic development, which has led some municipalities to offer skills programmes. In Stellenbosch, for example, the municipality-sponsored Youth Skills Development Programme offers accredited skills training programmes to a number of unemployed youth. Similarly, the city of Cape Town provides programmes and workshops to support young job seekers, including employment and work readiness skills, organisational capacity building, life skills and career guidance.

Box 4.1. Tshepo 1 Million –Training and job opportunities for unemployed youth in Gauteng

In 2014, the Gauteng provincial government launched the Tshepo 500 000 programme, aimed at training, skilling and mentoring 500 000 youth in the period 2014-19. The target was increased to 1 million in 2017, renaming the programme Tshepo 1 Million. In the first three years of the programme, 450 000 young people participated. The four key focus areas of the programme are:

- Demand-led learning: skills development related to verifiable market demand
- Transitional placements: Paid work done on a temporary basis aimed at developing work experience and/or sector specific skills
- Decent jobs: Paid work on contract at or above the sectoral minimum wage for full-time work, preferably permanent
- New economy/SMMEs: Facilitation of young entrepreneurs establishing and operating new enterprises/franchises

Part of the project is the mass digital learning system that is hosted in government sites, such as libraries, school and community centres. The system provides video learning for various types of opportunities, including the Matric re-write. The system also includes the Microsoft Thinti'Imillion initiative, a desktop and phone application designed to teach Microsoft Word, Excel and Powerpoint to people who have never used a computer.

An important part of the programme is the profiling of candidates, for which a partnership with Harambee Youth Employment Accelerator is set up. This partnership manages the pathway of each young jobseeker who enters the programme via a series of interventions, matching each entrant to the most viable pathway based on their skills profile, geography, learning potential, aptitudes, level of self-management and other relevant personal factors. When selected for a specific pathway, participants will often receive bridging and competency training to move them from their current situation to where the opportunity requires them to be in terms of capabilities, work-readiness, behaviours and work-habits.

To facilitate the creation of internship opportunities for youth in the province, the Tshepo 1 Million project benefits from a strong and growing network of business relationships. The programme also supports the growth of SMMEs, through cooperation with the Youth Employment Services (YES), the CEO initiative and Business Leadership South Africa, so that internships can also be created in smaller and informal businesses.

Source: Gauteng Province Office of the Premier (2017[7]; 2018[8]; 2018[9])

Recommended action steps

Table 4.1 provides some possible action steps that could be taken to obtain or channel funding from the central, provincial and/or municipal government budgets for CET. For each action step, the most relevant stakeholders concerned are listed. The list of stakeholders is not exhaustive, and cooperation between different stakeholders is encouraged. The actions steps focus on the short- and medium-term, and a more ambitious action plan could be developed for the longer term in line with the vision for CET from the DHET's strategic documents.

Table 4.1. Action steps for government financing

Action steps and relevant stakeholders

Action steps	Main stakeholders
Coordinate closely with the provincial and municipal governments to understand the training programmes they fund/offer. Make sure they understand that CET could be a potential provider of their training programmes.	CET Colleges, CLCs, municipal & provincial government
Submit a concrete and realistic funding request with the Treasury. A positive answer from the Treasury is more likely when the request concerns concrete plans that have clear political support.	DHET

The National Skills Fund should become a key contributor to CET development

The National Skills Fund (NSF) was established in 1999 by the National Skills Development Act, with the goal to provide funding for national skills priorities. The NSF is funded through the skills development levy, which allocates 20% of the funds collected from employers to the NSF (see Chapter 1). Since 2014/15 the NSF also receives the uncommitted surpluses of SETAs. In the financial year 2016/17, the NSF received just over ZAR 3 billion in levy payments. The NSF spends its funds in four broad areas: i) education and training, ii) post-school education and training system development and capacity building, iii) "no fee increase"[3], and iv) skills development research, innovation and communication. Spending by the NSF increased substantially in the last years, reaching ZAR 5 billion in 2016/17 (Figure 4.1). Spending on education and training accounted for 47% of total expenditure, benefitting 48 169 learners. The largest part of the budget for education and training was spent on higher education (57%), although the largest number of learners (52%) were in workplace-based training. The number of learners benefiting from NSF funding has decreased substantially over the years, and now reaches less than half of the number of learners in 2011/12. The strong decline can partially be attributed to the NSFs contribution to the "no fee increase" in recent years, but also to a stronger focus on infrastructure development.

According to the third National Skills Development Strategy, the NSF should enable the state to drive key skills strategies as well as to meet the training needs of the unemployed, non-levy-paying cooperatives, NGOs and community structures and vulnerable groups. Among the key priorities identified in the Strategy are "Addressing the low level of youth and adult language and numeracy skills to enable additional training", as well as "Encouraging and supporting cooperatives, small enterprises, worker-initiated, NGO and community training initiatives". These objectives are in line with the envisaged goal of the CET system. Given that the NSF's mandate is to fund skills priorities and training of the unemployed and vulnerable groups, it should play a key role in the financing of the CET system. Notwithstanding, in the last years, the largest part of NSF funding has been targeted toward university education, as higher education received the majority of education and training funding, as well as large sums for system development and capacity building. In addition, 35% of the total NSF skills development expenditure in 2016/17 was for the "no fee increase" in universities and TVET colleges.

Figure 4.1. The National Skills Fund plays an important role in funding skill development

Expenditure, assets and beneficiaries

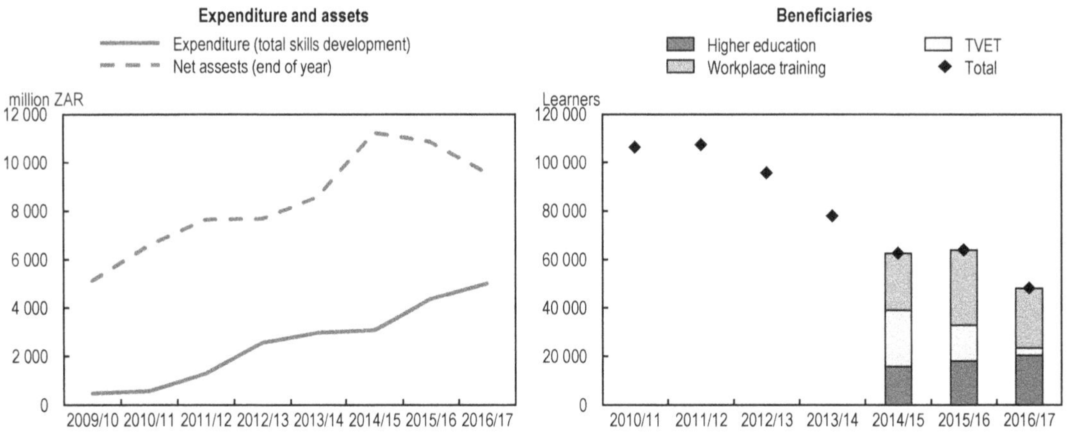

Note: Total expenditure only refers to skills development expenditure, and does not include expenditure on NSF operations.
Source: NSF annual reports, Department for Higher Education and Training (2016[10]; 2011[11]).

As Figure 4.1 shows, the NSF has built up large reserves over the years, because of underspending in initial years, as well as the transfer of SETA surpluses in recent years. The 2016/17 NSF annual report notes that the NSF has committed and earmarked its entire reserve and accumulated surplus towards skills development programmes and projects. The majority of the already committed funding is for post-school education and training system development and capacity building (63%).

Recommended action steps

Table 4.2 provides some possible action steps that could be taken to obtain additional funding from the National Skills Fund for CET. For each action step, the most relevant stakeholders concerned are listed. The list of stakeholders is not exhaustive, and cooperation between different stakeholders is encouraged. The actions steps focus on the short- and medium-term, and a more ambitious action plan could be developed for the longer term in line with the vision for CET from the DHET's strategic documents.

Table 4.2. Actions steps for NSF funding

Action steps and relevant stakeholders

Action steps	Main stakeholders
Re-focus the NSF so that it is better targeted at the unemployed and other disadvantaged groups.	DHET
Earmark a substantial part of the NSF annual budget for CET investment	DHET
Re-evaluate the already earmarked funds for the medium-term, so that the NSF can be mobilised as soon as possible for CET funding	DHET

Note: DHET: Department for Higher Education and Training.

Sector Education and Training Authorities need to spend their funds more efficiently

Sector Education and Training Authorities (SETAs) are key players in the South African skills development system. By redistributing the skills development levy (see Chapter 1), they fund training opportunities for a large group of employed and unemployed individuals. In the financial year 2016/17, SETAs received ZAR 12.2 billion levy income. Using SETA funding, 130 353 workers and 114 230 unemployed entered into skills programmes and learnerships or received bursaries. In addition, the funds were used to support non-governmental and community organisations, and to provide career guidance. SETA levy revenues are expected to increase to ZAR 15.855 billion by 2020/21. SETAs on the whole experienced surpluses during most years up to 2015/16. This can be ascribed to: i) mandatory grants not having been claimed by employers; ii) intended grant beneficiaries not having met the criteria that would have made them eligible for funding; iii) the fact that resources are committed for a longer time horizon; and iv) a weak implementation culture in SETAs (Department of Higher Education and Training, 2016[12]). As mentioned above, in recent years surpluses have been transferred to the National Skills Fund.[4]

Every year, the Department for Higher Education and Training (DHET) concludes service level agreements with the SETAs. These agreements set targets in ten areas: i) administration; ii) research and skills planning; iii) occupationally directed programmes; iv) TVET college programmes; v) low level youth and adult language and numeracy skills; vi) workplace-based skills development; vii) support to co-ops, small enterprises, NGOs and worker initiated/community training initiatives; viii) administration and public sector capacity; ix) career and vocational guidance; and x) medium-term strategic priorities. As Figure 4.2 shows, the targets for the different types of training programmes across all SETAs have remained relatively stable in recent years. Targets for certain programmes even declined in the last year. Actual participation increased gradually in all programmes. To ensure that SETAs remain committed to invest in skills development, ambitious targets need to be set, especially in light of growing funds from the skills development levy and underspending of SETAs. At the same time, the performance of SETAs should not only be measured in terms of training quantity, but also training quality.

Figure 4.2. SETA training targets have remained relatively stable in recent years

Evolution of training targets and training enrolments (2011-18)

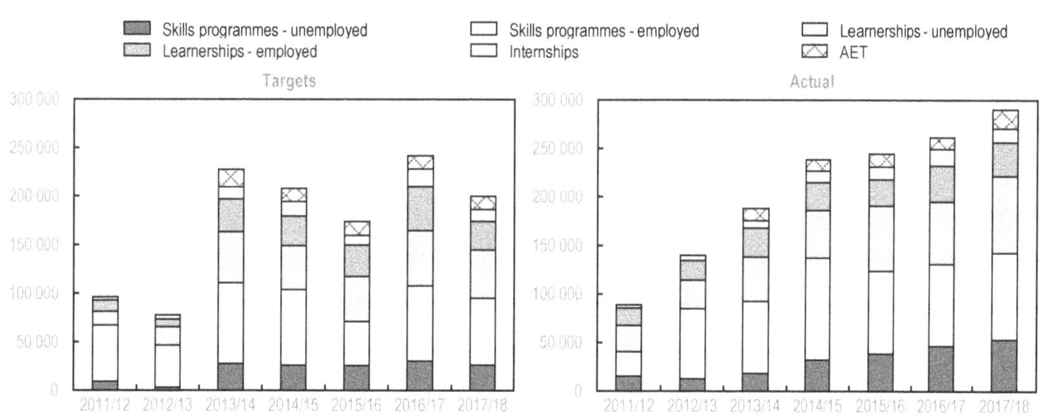

Note: All SETAs combined.
Source: Department for Higher Education and Training.

Figure 4.3 shows that targets for learnerships, skills programme, internships and second chance primary and secondary education (AET) registrations differ strongly between SETAs. In total, SETAs exceeded their target for learnerships for workers in 2017/18 by 29% and for the unemployed by 103%. For the skills programmes, the target was exceeded for workers by 19% and for the unemployed by 60%. Targets were also exceeded for internships (16%) and AET participation (43%). While targets were surpassed on average, there were some SETAs that did not manage to reach their targets.

Figure 4.3. Some SETAs have difficulties reaching their training targets

Number of workers and unemployed participating in SETA-supported learning programmes (2017/18)

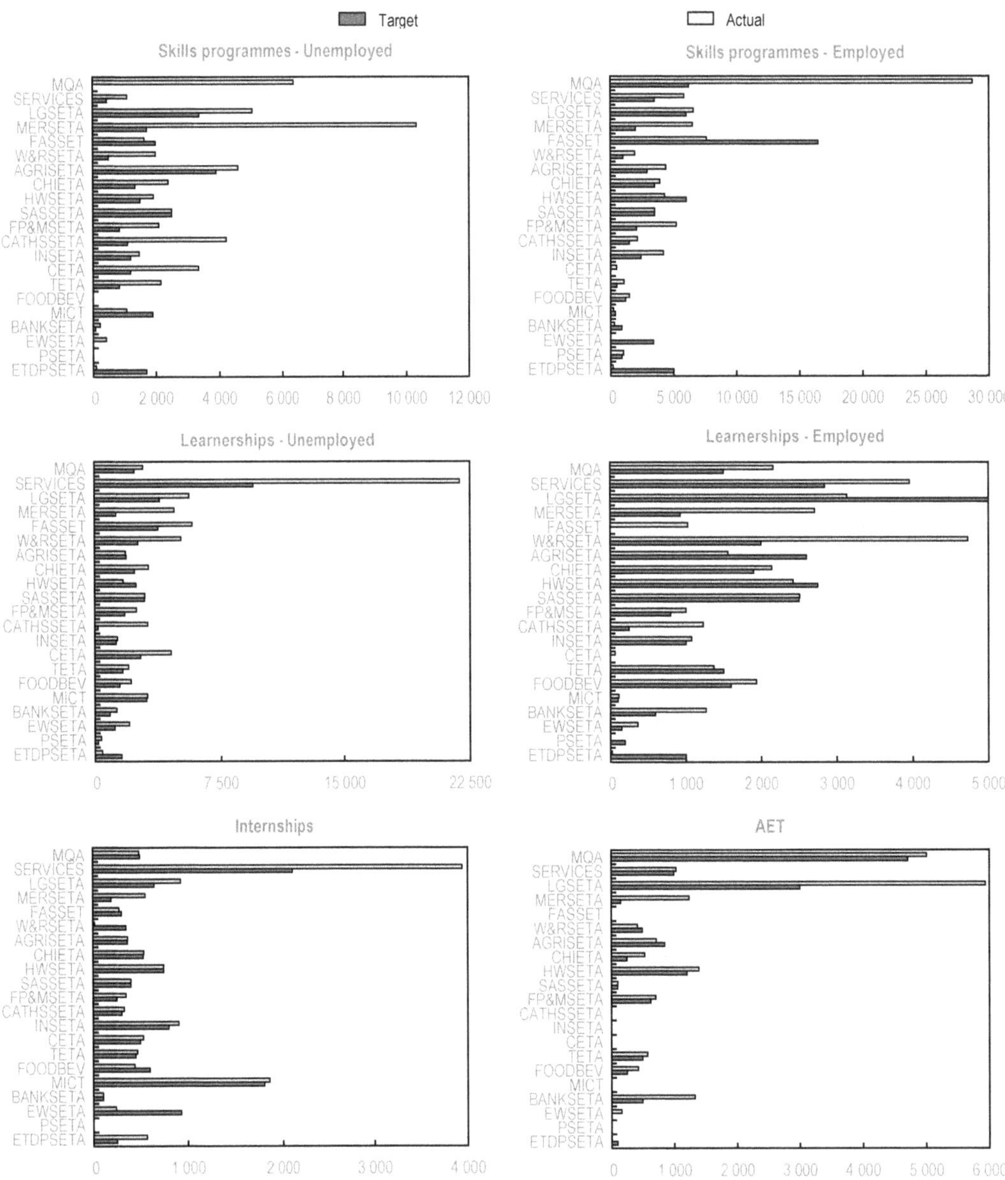

Note: SETAs are ranked in descending order by the total number of participants (all programmes combined)
Source: Department of Higher Education and Training.

Recommended Action steps

Table 4.3 provides some possible action steps that could be taken to channel funding from the skills development levy to CET. For each action step, the most relevant stakeholders concerned are listed. The list of stakeholders is not exhaustive, and cooperation between different stakeholders is encouraged. The actions steps focus on the short- and medium-term, and a more ambitious action plan could be developed for the longer term in line with the vision for CET from the DHET's strategic documents.

Table 4.3. Action steps for SETA funding

Action steps and relevant stakeholders

Action steps	Main stakeholders
Set more ambitious targets for SETA in terms of training, especially in light of the growing levy collection and the consistent underspending.	DHET
Make all the basic skills and second change programmes, vocational skills programmes and non-formal job-related programmes in CET eligible for PIVOTAL funding. Similarly, make internships for graduates from CET vocational skills programmes eligible for SETA funding.	DHET, SETAs
Make sure that SETAs coordinate closely with the CET system, such that CET institutions become a key provider of SETA-funded programmes (when there are no already established providers in the community) and have up-to-date information on SETA training programmes in their region.	SETAs, CLCs, CET Colleges
Improve the overall SETA system, including more transparency (e.g. on target setting, on the allocation of funds), lower administrative burden for claiming the mandatory and discretionary grants, and capacity building for SETAs to improve their data collection and analysis skills as well as knowledge on the accreditation of skills programmes.	DHET, SETAs

Note: DHET: Department for Higher Education and Training; SETA: Sector Education and Training Authority; CLC: Community Learning Centre.

Other potential funding sources need to be considered

The Unemployment Insurance Fund could expand its funding of training opportunities

Employers and workers contribute to the Unemployment Insurance Fund (UIF), each at a rate of 1% of the workers' monthly pay. The Fund is used to provide short-term relief to workers when they become unemployed or unable to work. Unemployed individuals can claim unemployment benefits at labour centres only if they are registered as job seekers. They need to return to the labour centre every four weeks to confirm unemployment status. Individuals who have contributed to the fund for a continuous period of at least four years can have access to benefits for the maximum duration of 365 days, others receive one day of benefits for each five days worked and contributed to the UIF. The Fund pays a percentage of the wage earned while contributing, with a maximum of 58%. In the financial year 2016/17, 763 000 valid claims were received. With a total number of unemployed individuals in the same period equal to around 6 011 000, this translates into a coverage rate of roughly 12.7%. According to Bhorat, Goga and Tseng (2016[13]) the relatively stringent rules of the South African unemployment insurance system exclude many vulnerable groups, such as informal workers, individuals without work experience and individuals in unstable jobs. The relatively low replacement rates, at least compared to OECD countries on average, potentially also make it not seem worthwhile for job seekers to claim their benefits.

In the financial year 2016/17, the revenues of the fund equalled ZAR 18.25 billion, and benefit payment amounted to ZAR 8.47 billion. As revenues have been exceeding benefit payments in most years, the UIF has been able to accumulate a substantial reserve (ZAR 139.5 billion in 2016/17).[5] In view of making better use of the available funds, the latest amendment of the Unemployment Insurance Act (2015) specified that the UIF funds can also be used for "financing of the retention of contributors in employment and the re-entry of contributors into the labour market and any other scheme aimed at vulnerable workers". This amendment makes it possible for the UIF to fund training programmes for contributing workers and job seekers. For the financial year 2017/18, the UIF set aside funding to train at least 6 000 individuals. To deliver the training, the Department of Labour collaborates with accredited public training providers (public higher education institutions, public TVET colleges, public entities and state owned enterprises) and SETAs. The Department launches an expression of interest for these institutions to submit proposals for apprenticeships, learnerships, unit standards based skills programmes, and new venture creating programmes. Training programmes can be either fully funded by the UIF or co-funded.

In most OECD countries, the responsibility of helping job seekers into employment lies with the Public Employment Service (PES). An international survey showed that in 70 out of 73 participating countries, PES provide a range of active labour market programmes to improve the employment outcomes of job-seekers (IDB, WAPES, OECD, 2015[14]). These active support measures often include skills development programmes. While the PES in most cases are not the direct providers of the training programmes, they do select available training programmes and provide funding. As the ultimate goal of PES is to help job seekers into sustained employment, they generally provide training programmes that are aligned with the needs of employers in the local labour market. In a range of countries, contributions to unemployment insurance are used to finance these and other activities of the PES. To make the most effective use of often-limited financial resources, some countries have put in place comprehensive profiling tools to better allocate resources to different groups of job seekers (see Box 4.2).

The Expanded Public Works and Community Works Programmes need a training component

In order to create job opportunities and to provide poverty and income relief for the low-skilled unemployed, the South African Department for Public Works launched the Expanded Public Works Programme (EPWP) in 2004. The participants are mainly placed in public sector funded infrastructure projects, but also in the environment and culture sector, the social sector, and in non-state projects. During the first phase of the programme (2004-09), 1.6 million work opportunities were created through the EPWP, and in the second phase (2009-14) opportunities increased to 4.3 million. The duration of the job opportunities in the second phase was limited to an average of 65 days. The participants were mainly unemployed individuals with some or completed secondary education, 50% of them being youth and 60% female. The third phase set a target of 6 million workplace opportunities by 2019, focussing the programme more strongly on youth.

Box 4.2. Targeting training interventions to the most vulnerable job-seekers

Many Public Employment Services (PES) across the world fund and/or provide training opportunities to registered job seekers. Active labour market policies, which include training, often account for the largest share of the PES budget. While public funding is the main source of financing for Active Labour Market Programmes around the world, unemployment insurance contributions are used as additional funding in many countries. As budgets for these programmes are often limited, PES generally target their training and other active interventions towards those job-seekers that are most in need of substantial help. In many OECD countries, PES use profiling tools to identify the most vulnerable job seekers who could benefit most from participation in training activities. The primary goal of profiling is to segment job seekers into homogenous groups in order to differentiate and better target PES interventions. Profiling generally takes three forms: i) based on caseworkers judgement, ii) following predetermined rules (e.g. related to unemployment duration or age of the job seeker), and iii) statistical profiling using data.

The Australian Job Seeker Classification Instrument

In Australia, registered job seekers are allocated to different streams based on their probability of remaining on income support for the following 12 months. This probability is estimated using a wide range of factors that affect an individual's difficulty in gaining and maintaining employment. These factors are:

- Age and gender
- Recency of work experience
- Job seeker history
- Educational attainment
- Vocational qualifications
- English proficiency
- Country of birth
- Indigenous status
- Indigenous location
- Geographic location
- Proximity to a labour market
- Access to transport
- Phone contactability
- Disability/medical conditions
- Stability of residence
- Living circumstances
- Criminal convictions
- Personal Factors

Each factor is given a weight, which is used for the aggregation into a final individual score for each jobseeker. Job seekers with higher scores are classified into streams with higher intensity of active labour market interventions.

Ireland's Probability of Exit Tool

Following the significant rise in unemployment during the Global Financial Crisis, Ireland moved away from its rules-based profiling, which only referred to job seekers to the PES after six months of unemployment, towards a statistical profiling system. The profiling tool estimates an individual's probability of exiting the unemployment register within twelve months. A job seeker's probability, referred to as the PEX score, not only depends on personal characteristic, but also on demand-side factors, proxied by geographical location and size of the location. The PEX score is used to classify job seekers as high-risk, medium-risk or low-risk, which determines the types of engagement and intensity of support. PES caseworkers still maintain a high degree of discretion in deciding which activation services to offer.

Source: Loxha and Morgandi (2014[15]), OECD (2012[16]; 2018[17]; 2015[18]), Australian Government - Department of Jobs and Small Business (2018[19]), Barnes et al. (2015[20]).

The non-state part of the EPWP was introduced in the second phase of the programme, and is mainly operationalised through the Community Works Programme (CWP). While CWP is a national programme co-ordinated by the Department of Cooperative Governance, it is implemented by non-profit agencies. The work in the CPW must be useful, defined as contributing to the public good and/or improving the quality of life in communities. The useful work concept is very broad, and contains areas such as food security, community care, support to early childhood development centres and to schools, and community safety. The programme is mainly implemented in rural areas, informal settlements and urban townships. (OECD, 2017[21])

As the EPWP and CWP are able to reach large groups of low-skilled unemployed South Africans, it provides a good opportunity to offer training in addition to work experience. Through funding from the Department for Higher Education and Training and SETAs, the programme already offers training to some of the participants, but this has been fairly limited. CET institutions could offer short-term training programmes to strengthen the skills of EPWP/CWP participants. These skills programmes could be targeted to the skills required in the EPWP/CWP jobs, but could also focus on general basic and employability skills. Including a training component in the EPWP/CWP could help participants to perform better in their assigned jobs, but also in improving their labour market prospects at the end of their EPWP/CWP participation.

Tuition fees could be charged, depending on students' income

In the current CET system, training programmes are in principle free for students. Nonetheless some of the CET centres charge minimal fees to cover specific costs, such as electricity and photocopying (Land and Aitchison, 2017[22]). As argued by both Land and Aitchison (2017[22]) and the Ministerial Committee on the review of funding frameworks of TVET and CET colleges (2017[23]), tuition fees should be avoided in the CET system, given that the target group generally consists of low-income students.

It could be envisaged that students bear part of the cost of CET programmes, provided that their income is high enough. In that case, a similar system as in TVET colleges or universities could be put in place. Some OECD countries have set up a system in which specific target groups receive vouchers that they can use to pay for training. In Estonia, for example, registered job seekers can access training opportunities through a system of training vouchers (*Koolituskaart*). These training vouchers have recently also been made available for certain groups of employees under specific conditions. In the case of low-wage older workers and low-skilled workers, the condition to use the training vouchers is that the training has to be related to ICT skills or skills identified as being in shortage by the Estonian Qualifications Authority.

The introduction of income-contingent tuition fees can only happen after a thorough analysis of the characteristics of CET students. If the system only attracts low-income students, setting up a tuition system would be unnecessary. However, if the CET system also attracts a substantial number of higher income students, a carefully designed tuition system could be introduced. It should be ensured that these tuition fees do not constitute a barrier for adults in need of training.

Cooperation with NGOs and social impact investors to obtain additional funding

A host of NGOs are active in South Africa in areas related to community education and training, including skills development programmes for adults and youth, matching job seekers to job opportunities, and career guidance. While they often operate on a small scale, their resources and knowledge could support the development and delivery of CET programmes. The Catholic Institute for Education, for example, operates multiple adult learning centres, which do not only offer basic literacy and numeracy programmes, but also skills programmes (OECD, 2017[21]). Another interesting example is Harambee, which matches young job seekers to employers, providing short skills development programmes when needed.

External donors are funding multiple skills development projects in South Africa, and more funding could be attracted to invest in skills development, including in CET. Social impact investment is increasingly being seen worldwide as a way to mobilise funds to tackle social issues. According to OECD (2015[24]), social impact investment has become increasingly relevant in today's economic setting as social challenges have mounted while public funds in many countries are under pressure. New approaches are needed for addressing social and economic challenges, including new models of public and private partnership that can fund, deliver and scale innovative solutions from the ground up. Social impact investors seek social and environmental impact from their investments, in addition to financial returns. Education, training and unemployment are key areas in which social impact investment can be mobilised. Vibrant entrepreneurial markets and strong enabling environments are crucial for facilitating this type of investment, as is the capacity to effectively measure outcomes (Wilson, 2016[25]).

Recommended action steps

Table 4.4 provides some possible action steps that could be taken to attract funding to CET from sources such as the unemployment insurance fund, the expanded public works programme and NGOs. For each action step, the most relevant stakeholders concerned are listed. The list of stakeholders is not exhaustive, and cooperation between different stakeholders is encouraged. The actions steps focus on the short- and medium-term, and a more ambitious action plan could be developed for the longer term in line with the vision for CET from the DHET's strategic documents.

Table 4.4. Action steps for other funding

Action steps and relevant stakeholders

Action steps	Main stakeholders
Allocate a larger part of the UIF surplus to training expenditure as a way to improve labour market entry of job-seekers	DoL
Open the expression for interest for UIF-funded training to CET, and make all CET training programmes eligible (academic second chance, vocational skills and non-formal job-related).	DoL
Give job-seekers who are most in need of up-skilling preferential access to the UIF-funded training opportunities	DoL, Labour Centres
Ensure that EPWP has a training component that is job-specific (delivered by CET or other training providers) or general (e.g. basic skill or employability skills, delivered by CET).	DHET, Departments of Public Works, Social Development, and Environmental Affaires
Explore possible funding from and cooperation with NGOs and external donors to provide training for low-skilled adults within the CET system or externally.	DHET, CET Colleges, CLCs, NGOs,
Make sure that the right conditions are in place to attract and facilitate social impact investment.	Several government departments

Note: DHET: Department for Higher Education and Training; DoL: Department of Labour; CLC: Community Learning Centre; NGO: Non-governmental organisation.

4.3. Priority funding areas

Poor infrastructure in Community Learning Centres limits their further development

Inadequate infrastructure is often said to be one of the big challenges for the quality, attractiveness and further development of the CET system. Most Community Learning Centres operate from (primary or secondary) school premises and share facilities with the schools. This means that the centres' operations are restricted by school operating hours (i.e. they can only provide training after school hours, when the facilities are not used for primary or secondary education), but also that many of the facilities are not adult-friendly. This setup restricts the possibility of centres developing into real community centres. While locating Community Learning Centres in schools is not a problem in itself, and there are in fact several benefits to this approach (e.g. efficient use of resources and visibility of CET), the centres should have a dedicated space in schools rather than using classrooms that are used for primary or secondary education during school hours.

It is unlikely that the CET system will be able to have a large enough budget in the short run to build new learning centres in all communities that do not have their own CET infrastructure. A better use of the limited funding would be to improve unused buildings or spare capacity in buildings such as TVET colleges or public libraries.

Expanding the role of CET to also provide vocational skills programmes will require investment in specialised training equipment. In light of the limited budget, but also the fact that the CET system should be flexible and responsive to local needs, investment in expensive equipment that is specific to certain training programmes should be minimised. Instead, CET institutions can enter into partnerships with other training providers (e.g. public TVET colleges, technical high schools, private training providers) and employers who already have the necessary equipment. The Gauteng government, for example, uses the equipment of public libraries for their digital skills programme (see Box 4.1).

If the current CET institutions want to transition into real community centres, some investment will certainly be required to make the centres more attractive. While the existing and potential new funding sources could contribute to these investments, CET institutions should also actively engage with potential donors, such as foundations, international organisations or development cooperation. Funds could be attracted to finance, for example, free Wi-Fi connection in the learning centres.

Recommended action steps

Table 4.5 provides some possible action steps that could be taken to the infrastructure in the CET system. For each action step, the most relevant stakeholders concerned are listed. The list of stakeholders is not exhaustive, and cooperation between different stakeholders is encouraged. The actions steps focus on the short- and medium-term, and a more ambitious action plan could be developed for the longer term in line with the vision for CET from the DHET's strategic documents.

Table 4.5. Action steps for improving CET infrastructure

Action steps and relevant stakeholders

Action steps	Main stakeholders
Analyse/audit the availability of empty spaces in communities where CET now operates in poor conditions.	Municipal government, CET Colleges, CLCs
Verify whether TVET colleges and higher education institutions have spare capacity to host Community Learning Centres or some of their training courses. Agreements to use their infrastructure should be formalised through standard contracts.	DHET, CET Colleges, CLCs, TVET colleges, universities, technical high schools
Encourage CET institutions to make agreements with private training providers and employers to use their rooms and equipment (following standard contracts)	DHET, CET Colleges, CLCs
Invest in making the Community Learning Centres an attractive space to learn and get together (e.g. comfortable meeting areas, free Wi-Fi)	DHET, CET Colleges, CLCs

Note: DHET: Department for Higher Education and Training; CLC: Community Learning Centre.

More and better trained staff is needed in the CET system

The national public budget for CET is almost entirely reserved for expenditure on compensation of employees. Timely payment of decent salaries for teachers in CET is crucial to attract and retain high-quality teachers (see Chapter 6). Therefore, sufficient funding for teacher salaries should be guaranteed. At the same time, the planned expansion of the system, both in terms of number of students and types of programmes, will require hiring a large number of new teachers. In an expanded CET system, the management of the CET institutions also becomes increasingly important, and management personnel will need to be recruited, as well as support staff.

As CET will gradually be taking up new roles, teachers, managers and support staff will have to learn how to provide these new functions. School managers must learn, for example, how to engage with local stakeholders. Teachers might need to learn how to deliver employability training programmes or vocational skills programmes. The support staff must learn how to register students and how to organise events (such as seminars on life skills). At the same time, lifelong learning becomes increasingly important for school personnel, especially if programmes and services need to be relevant and up to date with community needs. Chapter 6 provides more details on how to ensure the quality of CET staff.

Recommended action steps

Table 4.6 provides some possible action steps that could be taken to ensure that the CET systems has sufficient and well-trained staff. For each action step, the most relevant stakeholders concerned are listed. The list of stakeholders is not exhaustive, and cooperation between different stakeholders is encouraged. The actions steps focus on the short- and medium-term, and a more ambitious action plan could be developed for the longer term in line with the vision for CET from the DHET's strategic documents.

Table 4.6. Action steps for investment in staff

Action steps and relevant stakeholders

Action steps	Main stakeholders
Review the staffing in CET institutions and hire additional staff where needed.	CLCs, CET Colleges, DHET
Develop training courses to get current CET staff members (e.g. teachers, management and support staff) ready for their new tasks and roles (see Chapter 6).	DHET, CET Colleges, TVET colleges, Universities
Set up an information system that keeps track of the training CET staff has participated in. This will help ensure that staff participates regularly in training to keep their skills up to date.	DHET, CET Colleges
Set up a platform to share good practices between CET staff members, especially concerning new tasks, such as forming partnerships with the private sector. This platform can be shared with TVET colleges, where many of the staff members are facing similar challenges	DHET, CET Colleges

Note: DHET: Department for Higher Education and Training; CLC: Community Learning Centre.

Teaching and training materials adapted to the needs of adults need to be developed

Programmes for adults need to be flexible, and allow for part-time and modular approaches that are consistent with other calls on their time. Easing time arrangements and providing flexible alternatives– with recognition of prior learning for example, have been successful in raising participation in several countries. These flexible approaches will also help students that have dropped out at some point to find their way back into the CET system with relatively low barriers. The Mexican basic education programme Model for Life and Work (*Modelo Educación para la Vida y el Trabajo*) is a flexible programme that allows participants to combine different modules at different levels (see Box 4.3).

As discussed in Chapter 3, teaching and learning materials in CET should ideally be adapted to adults. This is particularly important for literacy and second chance education materials, which are often taken from or based on materials from basic education. Instead, these materials should relate to situations that adults come across in daily life, so that it is directly applicable to their lives. The Kha Ri Gude campaign was able to develop this type of adapted materials. Adult learners do not acquire skills in the same way as children, and research shows that teaching methods that work for children may not do so for adults (German Federal Ministry for Education and Research, 2012[26]) (MacArthur et al., 2012[27]). For example, most adults who want to improve their literacy and numeracy skills already have a range of skills and almost all of them can read or write to some extent (Wells, 2001[28]). Formative assessment, which implies adapting instruction to learner needs by means of regular assessment and tracking learning progress, may be a particularly effective tool for adult learning (see Box 4.4).

TVET colleges or other training providers can share their materials to be used for vocational skills programmes in CET. Similarly, materials from non-formal programmes can be developed following the example from other providers or stakeholders (e.g. from employers providing employability skills training, see Chapter 3).

Digital learning materials provide an opportunity to reach a large group of individuals, provided they have access to digital technologies and have basic digital skills. CET institutions could make digital technologies available to adults who do not have their own computer, tablet or smartphone, and could provide basic digital skills programmes to individuals lacking the skills to use digital resources. Within their Tshepo 1 Million programme, the Gauteng province partnered with Microsoft to make digital resources available for adults to learn how to use Microsoft office software (see Box 4.1). The Mexican basic education programme Model for Life and Work (*Modelo Educación para la Vida y el Trabajo*) allows participants to complete some of the modules online (see Box 4.3). Evidence from a sample of CET students shows that access to technology is the main feature that students would have liked added to the CET support services (Lolwana, Rabe and Morakane, 2018[29]).

Box 4.3. Flexible basic education for youth and adults in Mexico

The Model for Life and Work programme (*Modelo Educación para la Vida y el Trabajo, MEVyT*) in Mexico provides learning opportunities for youth and adults to catch up on primary and secondary education. The programme integrates basic literacy learning with skills training and allows the learners to obtain officially recognised and accredited primary and secondary qualifications. The programme is very flexible, allowing participants to select different modules at the initial, intermediate (primary education) and advanced (lower secondary education) level. The modules cover a wide range of topics, including civic education, language and communication, mathematics and science, social development and citizenship. Some modules also have a focus on the world of work, such as "My business" and "Working in harmony".

The modular structure of the programme allows learners to design their own curriculum by selecting modules according to their prior skills, needs, interests and the speed at which they learn. This flexibility also allows learners to decide when, where and how they want to learn. Individuals can study on their own or participate in group learning in a community learning centre or a mobile learning space.

To allow for even greater flexibility, an online version of the programme was introduced. Students can participate in a range of modules on an online platform (*MEVyT en linea*). The platform currently mainly provides the basic modules (i.e. language and communication, mathematics and science) at the intermediate and advanced level, but also a few of the diversified modules (e.g. parenting, the prevention of violence). To help individuals with low digital skills access the online training modules, basic digital skills programmes are offered in community learning centres.

Source: Unesco Institute for Lifelong Learning (2016[30]); Instituto Nacional para la Educacion de los Adultos (2018[31]).

Recommended action steps

Table 4.7 provides possible action steps that could be taken to ensure that the CET system has sufficient and high-quality teaching and learning materials. For each action step, the most relevant stakeholders concerned are listed. The list of stakeholders is not exhaustive, and cooperation between different stakeholders is encouraged. The actions steps focus on the short- and medium-term, and a more ambitious action plan could be developed for the longer term in line with the vision for CET from the DHET's strategic documents.

Table 4.7. Action steps for investment teaching and learning materials

Action steps and relevant stakeholders

Action steps	Main stakeholders
Develop integrated learning materials for the second chance programmes, based on the lessons learnt from the DBE-DHET literacy group (see Chapter 3).	DHET, DBE
Explore teaching methods that especially meet the needs of adults (e.g. contextualised learning and formative assessment).	DHET
Ensure all learning opportunities allow for flexible and modular approaches to address adults' time constraints and their potential need to complete programmes in multiple stages	DHET, CET Colleges, CLCs
Coordinate with TVET colleges to obtain the necessary teaching and learning materials for the vocational skills programmes.	DHET, CET Colleges, TVET colleges
Coordinate with employers, NGOs and government departments to obtain or develop teaching and learning materials for the non-formal programmes.	DHET, CET Colleges, Employers, NGOs, other government departments
Set up a task team that reviews existing online learning tools that could potentially be used in CET and develop new online materials.	DHET
Take stock of available IT resources (e.g. computers, tablets) in the community that could be used in CET institutions or be made accessible to CET students (e.g. libraries, enterprises).	CET Colleges, CLCs

Note: DHET: Department for Higher Education and Training; CLC: Community Learning Centre; DBE: Department for Basic Education.

Box 4.4. Elements of quality formative assessment

The OECD review *Teaching, Learning and Assessment for Adults* reviewed available English-language evidence on formative assessment and identified the following good practice elements:

- *Dialogue between teachers and learners*: teachers should structure learning as dialogue between themselves and their students.
- *Communication skills*: teachers need to evaluate and extend their communication skills, particularly focusing on listening, understanding, asking questions, and giving feedback.
- *Feedback and marking*: feedback should focus on the task rather than the person, be constructive and practical, and be returned as soon as possible.
- *Developing an atmosphere conducive to learning*: students should feel secure to face challenges and take risks in asking questions that may reveal their lack of understanding.
- *Peer assessment and self-assessment*: self-assessment and peer-assessment should be central elements of all learning situations.
- *Collaborative learning activities*: discussions and collaborative activities have proven beneficial to many learners.

Source: OECD (2008[321])

A sound administration system is imperative for the functioning of CET institutions

To be able to monitor and evaluate the quality of the CET system, it will be imperative to have strong administrative systems in place that allow to collect information on registered students, completion rates, progression to further education and employment. Measuring the outcomes of training is not only important for quality measurement (see Chapter 6), but also for guaranteeing that training programmes respond to community needs (see Chapter 5). Using digital technology to collect and produce these data can significantly reduce the time and administrative cost allocated to monitoring and evaluation, as well as improve the quality of the evaluation exercises (Unesco, 2016[33]).

Moreover, as the CET system will build strongly on cooperation and partnerships with a wide range of stakeholders, strong administration will be important to formalise partnerships. For example, when a CET institution agrees to use equipment in TVET colleges, this agreement needs to be made official, and this requires sound administrative processes. Chapter 6 discusses how sound administration contributes to CET quality.

Recommended action steps

Table 4.8 provides possible action steps that could be taken to ensure that the CET system has sufficient administrative capacity to perform its tasks. For each action step, the most relevant stakeholders concerned are listed. The list of stakeholders is not exhaustive, and cooperation between different stakeholders is encouraged. The actions steps focus on the short- and medium-term, and a more ambitious action plan could be developed for the longer term in line with the vision for CET from the DHET's strategic documents.

Table 4.8. Action steps for investment in administrative capacity

Action steps and relevant stakeholders

Action steps	Main stakeholders
Develop a universal student registration system, so that all CET institutions collect the same information. Develop this as a digital tool (preferred mode) but also as a paper-based tool for institutions with limited digital resources.	DHET
Coordinate with other government departments on the required information to be able to link the CET data to other datasets (e.g. basic education, UIF).	DHET, other government departments
Develop standard contracts for partnerships between CET institutions and other stakeholders (e.g. to regulate the use of equipment).	DHET
Train management and support staff for their new tasks and for using new administrative tools.	DHET, CET Colleges, CLCs

Note: DHET: Department for Higher Education and Training; CLC: Community Learning Centre.

Notes

[1] The shortfall amounts to ZAR 16.88 billion in nominal terms, and ZAR 6.447 billion in real terms.

[2] The OECD projects real GDP growth to reach 0.7% in 2018 and 1.7% in 2019 (OECD, 2018[35]). Similarly, the International Monetary Fund (IMF) projects real GDP growth to reach 0.8% in 2018 and 1.4% in 2019, much lower than the average of emerging market and developing economies (4.7% in 2018 and 2019) (International Monetary Fund, 2018[34]).

[3] Following a series of student protests, the decision was taken not to increase fees for students from poor and working-class families in 2016 and cap increases in 2017. The NSF contributed additional funding to TVET colleges and universities to help alleviate the impact of the lower fee collection.

[4] The SETA grant regulations state that SETAs can only transfer 5% of their uncommitted surpluses to the next financial year. Exceptions can be granted by the Minister of Higher Education and Training. The remainders of the surpluses are transferred to the NSF. Following a court case against the transfer of SETA surpluses to the NSF (by Business Unity South Africa), this part of the grant regulations has been set aside by the Labour Appeal Court in November 2017. SETAs are now no longer expected to transfer their uncommitted surpluses to the NSF, and are urged by the Department for Higher Education and Training to spend all their funds on skills development initiatives in their relevant sectors.

[5] Of the total UIF assets in 2016/2017, 41.5% were listed as current assets, meaning that they can be converted into cash and operationalised within a relatively short time period (generally less than twelve months).

References

Australian Government - Department of Jobs and Small Business (2018), *Components of the Job Seeker Classification Instrument (JSCI)*, https://www.jobs.gov.au/components-and-results-job-seeker-classification-instrument (accessed on 1 June 2018). [19]

Barnes, S. et al. (2015), *Identification of latest trends and current developments in methods to profile jobseekers in European Public Employment Services: Final report*, European Commission. [20]

Bhorat, H., S. Goga and D. Tseng (2016), "Unemployment Insurance in South Africa: A descriptive overview of claimants and claims", *Africa Growth Initiative*, No. 8, Brookings, https://www.brookings.edu/wp-content/uploads/2016/06/04_unemployment_insurance_south_africa.pdf (accessed on 22 May 2018). [13]

Department of Higher Education and Training (2016), *Investment trends in post-school education and training in South Africa*. [12]

Department of Higher Education and Training (2016), *Statistics on Post-School Education and Training in South Africa Statistics on Post-School Education and Training in South Africaa*, Department for Higher Education and Training. [10]

Department of Higher Education and Training (2011), *Annual Report 2010/2011*, Department for Higher Education and Training, Pretoria. [11]

DNA Economics (2016), *Volume 5: Consolidated Report on the Costing and Financing of the White Paper on PSET*, DNA Economics, Pretoria. [5]

FiBS and DIE (2013), *Developing the adult learning sector - Lot 2: Financing the Adult Learning Sector*, http://lll.mon.bg/uploaded_files/financingannex_en.pdf (accessed on 6 August 2018). [1]

Gauteng Government (2018), *Microsoft/ Tshepo1Million Thint'iMillion Initiative*. [9]

Gauteng Government (2018), *Tshepo 1Million: Primer*. [8]

Gauteng Government (2017), *Tshepo 1 Million programme profile*. [7]

German Federal Ministry for Education and Research (2012), *Alphabetisierung und Grundbildung Erwachsener: Abschlussdokumentation des Förderschwerpunktes zur Forschung und Entwicklung 2007-2012*, http://dx.doi.org/www.alphabund.de/1861.php. [26]

IDB, WAPES, OECD (2015), *The World of Public Employment Services*. [14]

Instituto nacional para la educacion de los adultos (2018), *MEVyT en línea*, http://mevytenlinea.inea.gob.mx/inicio/index.html (accessed on 13 July 2018). [31]

International Monetary Fund (2018), *World Economic Outlook - Challenges to Steady Growth*, IMF, Washington D.C., http://www.imfbookstore.org. [34]

Land, S. and J. Aitchison (2017), *The Ideal Institutional Model for Community Colleges in South Africa: A Discussion Document*, Durban University of TEchnology, Durban, https://www.dut.ac.za/wp-content/uploads/2017/06/Community-Colleges-in-South-Africa-September-2017.pdf (accessed on 17 January 2019). [22]

Lolwana, P., E. Rabe and M. Morakane (2018), "Who accesses adult education and where do they progress to? An exploratory tracer study in community education and training", *LMIP reports*, No. 37, Labour Market Intelligence Parternship, http://www.lmip.org.za/document/who-accesses-adult-education-and-where-do-they-progress-exploratory-tracer-study-community (accessed on 7 November 2018). [29]

Loxha, A. and M. Morgandi (2014), "Profiling the unemployed: A review of OECD experiences and implications for emerging economies", *Social Protection & Labor Discussion Paper*, No. 1424, World Bank, http://documents.worldbank.org/curated/en/678701468149695960/pdf/910510WP014240Box385327B0PUBLIC0.pdf (accessed on 31 May 2018). [15]

MacArthur, C. et al. (2012), "Reading component skills of learners in adult basic education", *Journal of Learning Disabilities*, Vol. Vol. 43(2), pp. pp. 108-121. [27]

Ministerial Committee on the review of the funding frameworks of TVET Colleges and CET colleges (2017), *Information Report and Appendices for presentation to Minister B.E. Nzimande, M.P.*. [23]

OECD (2019), *Getting Skills Right: Future-Ready Adult Learning Systems*, Getting Skills Right, OECD Publishing, Paris, https://dx.doi.org/10.1787/9789264311756-en. [2]

OECD (2018), *OECD Economic Outlook, Volume 2018 Issue 2*, OECD Publishing, Paris, https://dx.doi.org/10.1787/eco_outlook-v2018-2-en. [35]

OECD (2018), "Profiling tools for early identification of jobseekers who need extra support", *Policy Brief on Activation Policies*, OECD, Paris, http://www.oecd.org/employment/connecting-people-with-good-jobs.htm (accessed on 5 February 2019). [17]

OECD (2017), *Getting Skills Right: South Africa*, Getting Skills Right, OECD Publishing, Paris, http://dx.doi.org/10.1787/9789264278745-en. [21]

OECD (2017), *The Funding of School Education: Connecting Resources and Learning*, OECD Reviews of School Resources, OECD Publishing, Paris, http://dx.doi.org/10.1787/9789264276147-en. [4]

OECD (2015), "Activation policies for more inclusive labour markets", in *OECD Employment Outlook 2015*, OECD Publishing, Paris, https://dx.doi.org/10.1787/empl_outlook-2015-7-en. [18]

OECD (2015), *Social Impact Investment: Building the Evidence Base*, OECD Publishing, Paris, http://dx.doi.org/10.1787/9789264233430-en. [24]

OECD (2012), *Activating Jobseekers: How Australia Does It*, OECD Publishing, Paris, http://dx.doi.org/10.1787/9789264185920-en. [16]

OECD (2008), *Teaching, Learning and Assessment for Adults: Improving Foundation Skills*, OECD Publishing, Paris, http://dx.doi.org/10.1787/9789264039964-en. [32]

Statistics South Africa (2017), *Quarterly financial statistics of municipalities*, http://www.statssa.gov.za/publications/P9110/P9110December2017.pdf (accessed on 2 May 2018). [6]

UNESCO (2017), *Ensuring adequate, efficient and equitable finance in schools in the Asia-Pacific region*, Unesco Asia and Pacific Regional Bureau for Education, Bangkok, http://www.unesco.org/open-access/terms-use-ccbysa-en (accessed on 10 September 2018). [3]

Unesco (2016), *Designing effective monitoring and evaluation of education systems for 2030: A global synthesis of policies and practices*, http://www.unesco.org/new/fileadmin/MULTIMEDIA/HQ/ED/pdf/me-report.pdf (accessed on 13 July 2018). [33]

Unesco Institute for Lifelong Learning (2016), *Education Model for Life and Work, Mexico*, http://uil.unesco.org/case-study/effective-practices-database-litbase-0/education-model-life-and-work-mexico (accessed on 13 July 2018). [30]

Wells, A. (2001), "Basic Skills-25 Years on", *Adults Learning*, Vol. 12/10. [28]

Wilson, K. (2016), "Investing for social impact in developing countries", in *Development Co-operation Report 2016: The Sustainable Development Goals as Business Opportunities*, OECD Publishing, Paris, http://dx.doi.org/10.1787/dcr-2016-11-en. [25]

Chapter 5. Aligning Community Education and Training with local needs

To ensure that Community education and training is useful for participants, the training offer and content needs to reflect the needs of the community and the local labour market. The needs of communities can be diverse, and a holistic understanding of these needs can only be achieved when a variety of local stakeholders is engaged. This chapter presents ways to ensure that community education and training programmes are aligned with labour market needs, with a particular focus on the local stakeholders that should be involved in assessing these needs.

5.1. Background

For community education and training to have a useful impact on individuals' lives, local employers and communities more broadly, the programmes and services offered at CET institutions need to be aligned with the needs of the community. Evidence from Asian community learning centres shows that in many countries, the planning and operations of these centres are influenced more by national policies and programmes than by localised planning and programme development. Key interventions that are found to improve relevance include knowing where job opportunities are and matching programmes to these opportunities, collaborative programmes where community learning centres cooperate with local stakeholders, and taking into account feedback from learners (Unesco, 2016[1]).

In many countries, the education system has become more decentralised, partly in an effort to become more responsive to local needs. Evidence from the PISA survey shows that school systems that grant more autonomy to schools to define and elaborate their curricula and assessments tend to perform better than systems that do not grant such autonomy, provided that accountability mechanisms are in place (OECD, 2013[2]). However, as pointed out by Dyer and Rose (2005[3]), the success of decentralisation depends on many factors, including whether the local educators have the necessary capacities and leadership skills, and available support from higher-level government. Decentralised governance may support diversity, innovation and competition, but the downside is that it can also create confusion for students in the face of multiple pathways, while employers may find engagement in multiple contexts too burdensome. There may also be duplication of tasks, such as curriculum design and quality assurance.

In the case of vocational programmes, alignment with industry needs can be ensured by allowing employers and organised labour to be involved in setting the content of programmes. However, their level of engagement is often highly variable. Sometimes formal mechanisms to involve industry are lacking or ineffective, for example because the industrial bodies involved are not representative or because their voice is weak compared to that of other stakeholders (e.g. education and training institutions, government bodies). Low levels of engagement result in programmes that lack relevance to the labour market and are not trusted by employers.

For education institutions to be responsive to local needs, they need to have a good understanding of what and where these needs are. As highlighted by Unesco (2014[4]), local communities are invaluable for identifying local priorities, so that real issues can be addressed. Schools must therefore have access to relevant local information, and need to have the skills to collect and analyse this information. According to OECD (2018[5]), for education systems to develop the skills that students need to thrive and shape their world, curricula have to be adaptable and dynamic so that they can be updated and aligned with societal requirements and individual learner needs. It is important to involve teachers, students and other relevant stakeholders early in the development of the curriculum, to ensure their ownership for implementation.

5.2. Flexibility in programme offering and content

One of the main goal of community education and training should be to improve the livelihoods of participants, by responding to their needs. This includes facilitating access to labour market opportunities, but also improving general knowledge and skills for day-to-day activities and problems. Therefore, for community education and training to have the desired impact, it should be responsive to the needs of the communities in which it is operational. Education and training systems that are truly responsive to local needs generally have some degree of flexibility in deciding on which courses to offer and on the content of training programmes. Countries are using a number of tools to allow for the local tailoring of course content, including: i) designating local time within the curriculum; ii) setting national curriculum frameworks to be operationalised locally; iii) national accreditation for locally designed curricula; and iv) modularisation (see Box 5.1). As an example, the professional programmes in Fachschulen in Germany are established centrally (by the Länder), but the individual institutions can determine around 20% of the curriculum (OECD, 2014[6]).

Box 5.1. Tailoring course curricula to respond to local skill needs

Giving training providers flexibility to determine (part of) the curricula of training programmes allows for more responsiveness to local skills needs. Different strategies are used to introduce flexibility in training programmes, each with their own strengths and weaknesses.

Table 5.1. Strategies for flexibility in education and training programmes

Strategy	Strengths	Weaknesses
Setting aside specific curriculum time for local priorities: Specific amount of course time set aside for locally developed content.	- Allows for a balance between nationally and locally relevant curricula. - Creates space for employers and social partners to engage locally. - Supports transferability of qualifications.	- Contingent on providers and teachers having the adequate capacity to develop relevant local curricula. - Percentage of time decisions may be perceived as arbitrary.
National curriculum frameworks, operationalised locally: Nationally designed framework curriculum is "fleshed out" locally	- Allows for a balance between nationally and locally relevant curricula. - Creates space for employers and social partners to engage locally. - Supports transferability of qualifications.	- Contingent on providers and teachers having adequate capacities and partnerships to develop relevant local curricula.
Local design, national accreditation: Programme design is done locally, and then accredited according to nationally set standards and parameters.	- Allows for a large degree of local tailoring. - National standards can be set to ensure strategic design decisions are mad	- Potentially limits national coherence. - Contingent on providers and teachers having adequate capacities to develop relevant local curricula. - Can lead to local areas "reinventing the wheel".
Modularisation: VET programmes are broken into defined modules, allowing local actors to tailor which modules are provide	- Allows for a balance between nationally and locally relevant curricula.	- Combining different kinds of courses can be difficult in practice for providers.

Source: OECD (2016[7]).

Some of the training programmes offered in CET institutions are general in nature, meaning that they respond to skill needs that cut across different communities. These general programmes include, for example, the literacy and second chance programmes. While the content of these programmes should be adapted to the target audience of adult learners, it can broadly be the same in all CET institutions across the country.

Similarly, some of the non-formal programmes, like employability and entrepreneurship programmes (see Chapter 3), target skill needs that can be observed across the country. However, it can be useful to adapt parts of these programmes to local realities, such as the prevailing industries and occupations in the local area. Entrepreneurship programmes in CET institutions that are located in areas where the informal sector plays an important role, could be focused partially on the particular realities and challenges related to operating an informal business and ways to progress into the formal sector. Employability programmes can also benefit from some degree of flexibility: in communities with a large share of economic activity in the hospitality sector, for example, the employability skills programme could devote more attention to social interaction skills. These types of programmes could therefore be configured as 'partially flexible': part of the programme is fixed (determined by the central level), and the other part allows for flexibility to respond to community needs. The flexible component of these programmes would also allow for inviting community members, like entrepreneurs or youth with successful career pathways, to share their insights in the skills that are important in working life. The Department for Higher Education and Training (DHET) could develop optional modules that can be used by the CET institutions.

Other programmes, like vocational and life skills programmes, would benefit from a large degree of flexibility, as these should be truly respond to the needs of the community. CET institutions should have the freedom to decide which programmes to offer, in consultation with community members. For the vocational skills programmes, CET institutions have the flexibility to combine different unit standards to create a programme that corresponds to the needs of local employers. To avoid a proliferation of vocational skill programmes and ensure that the course offering responds to real community needs, a system can be set up in which Community Learning Centres need to submit requests for opening specific programmes, justifying why there is a need, with the CET College Manager (i.e. the manager of the provincial administrative hub of the CET system). This system would only work if CET Colleges have the capacity to respond without significant delays to these requests. Similarly, CET institutions should be able to decide on the content and form of some non-formal programmes, like life skills programmes, adapted to the needs of the participants. However, the DHET should make general teaching materials available for a range of common topics related to life skills. This can be done in cooperation with other Departments and NGOs.

Recommended action steps

Table 5.2 provides some possible action steps that could be taken to introduce flexibility in the programme offering at CET institutions. For each action step, the most relevant stakeholders concerned are listed. The list of stakeholders is not exhaustive, and cooperation between different stakeholders is encouraged. The actions steps focus on the short- and medium-term, and a more ambitious action plan could be developed for the longer term in line with the vision for CET from the DHET's strategic documents.

Table 5.2. Action steps for flexibility in programme offering

Action steps and relevant stakeholders

Action steps	Main stakeholders
Design curricula for the centrally determined (components of) training programmes, in consultation with key stakeholders.	DHET, SETAs, employers, DBE
Develop general teaching and learning materials for (the flexible part of) non-formal programmes, such as life skills and employability programmes. Existing materials from other stakeholders (e.g. NGOs, other ministries) can be used or serve as an input.	DHET, SETAs, employers, NGOs, other government departments
Train college and centre managers on understanding the unit standards system and on curriculum design. This should be done in cooperation with SETAs and TVET colleges.	DHET, CET Colleges, CLCs, SETAs, TVET colleges

Note: DHET: Department for Higher Education and Training; DBE: Department of Basic Education; CLC: Community Learning Centre; SETA: Sector Education and Training Authority; NGO: Non-Governmental Organisation; TVET: Technical and Vocational Education and Training.

5.3. Using available skill needs information

The identification of skills needs is not a straightforward exercise, and usually involves a wide range of tools and stakeholders (OECD, 2016[8]). In South Africa, information on labour market needs is available from multiple actors, at different levels of disaggregation. As argued by OECD (2017[9]), the available information on labour market needs is not used extensively in South Africa. In most OECD countries, skills needs information is used by policy-makers in the areas of employment, education and training, and migration, but also by social partners. Nonetheless, there are many reasons why skill needs data are not used as much as they could be, including insufficient sharing of the results with key stakeholders and the wider public, results that are too technical and/or not sufficiently disaggregated, and the fact that policies related to tackling skill needs are scattered across government levels and agencies (OECD, 2016[8]).

In South Africa, comprehensive skill needs exercises exist at different levels of disaggregation:

- *National level:* At the national level, the DHET produces every other year a list of occupations in high demand using both quantitative and qualitative information. In addition, the OECD's Skills for Jobs database provides information on the skills that are in shortage and surplus in South Africa's labour market. While these national level data might be too general to decide on training needs at the community level, they do provide relevant background information on the type of skills that are important in today's and tomorrow's labour market.
- *Sector level:* Part of the mandate of the SETAs is to determine skill needs in their respective sectors. Using information from employers in their sectors, SETAs annually produce sector skills plans, which contain information on the skills most in demand or shortage in the sector. This information is used to prioritise funding under the skills development levy system. The sector skills plans can help communities understand the skill needs of the main sectors in their local area. Moreover, SETAs could use the information gathered from employers to look at needs at the regional or local level.
- *Municipal level:* South African municipalities use integrated strategic planning to plan their future development. In cooperation with local stakeholders, municipalities develop 5-year integrated development plans, which can be revised annually. The first stage of the development of such a plan is the identification of community needs. These needs guide the development of a vision, objectives, strategies, and –ultimately- projects. It is recommended that municipalities set up a Representative Forum to facilitate and encourage the participation of local stakeholders. The Integrated Development Plans could provide valuable information on local needs to CET institutions.
- *Infrastructure project level:* Large public infrastructure projects create skill needs in specific regions or sectors. The DHET developed a tool to anticipate skill needs related to these infrastructure projects and find and/or train the necessary workers (OECD, 2017[9]). One of the steps in the tool is to consider schools in the local area to deliver the necessary training. When CET is truly responsive to local labour market needs, it could be the ideal provider of some of the training needed for the infrastructure projects.

A data source that is not used extensively in South Africa to analyse labour market needs is information from vacancies.[1] In many countries, vacancy data are used to analyse which skills and occupations are in demand in the labour market. In some countries, the number of vacancies is compared to the number of job seeker to calculate pressure on the labour market. In South Africa, the Department of Labour collects information on vacancies from newspapers for their annual report on job opportunities and unemployment, to understand the trends in demand for each occupation and industry. Private firms also provide information on vacancies in South Africa. CareerJunction, a platform for matching job seekers and vacancies, for example, publishes monthly reports on the evolution of demand and supply, highlighting the skills and occupations with the strongest demand. South Africa also has a public employment service, Employment Services South Africa (ESSA), which has a database of registered job seekers and vacancies. The information from vacancy data could be used to better understand demand in the local labour market. While data is generally disseminated at the national level, more disaggregate information could be made available for CET colleges and learning centres. At an international level, the use of web-scraping technologies to analyse online vacancies is becoming increasingly popular, as it allows getting real-time detailed information on available vacancies and their content. Such an analysis can be complementary to other vacancy collection exercises (e.g. from printed media), especially when the share of vacancies posted online is limited.

Recommended action steps

Table 5.2 provides some possible action steps that could be taken to collect and use skill needs information. For each action step, the most relevant stakeholders concerned are listed. The list of stakeholders is not exhaustive, and cooperation between different stakeholders is encouraged. The actions steps focus on the short- and medium-term, and a more ambitious action plan could be developed for the longer term in line with the vision for CET from the DHET's strategic documents.

Table 5.3. Action steps for collecting and using skill needs information

Action steps and relevant stakeholders

Action steps	Main stakeholders
Set up information sessions for CET staff to get familiar with existing skill needs data	DHET, CLCs, CET Colleges, SETAs, municipal government, DoL
Create a digital platform where all skill needs information is brought together	DHET
Explore ways to make better use of available vacancy information	DHET, DoL
Coordinate with SETAs and ESSA to obtain skills needs information at the local level	CLCs, CET Colleges, SETAs, Labour Centres

Note: DHET: Department for Higher Education and Training; CLC: Community Learning Centre; SETA: Sector Education and Training Authority; DoL: Department of Labour.

5.4. Involving key local stakeholders

In addition to consulting existing information on skill needs, the CET system should gather inputs directly from relevant local stakeholders. These stakeholders can help identifying key areas of skill needs, but also help in designing training programmes. At the same time, the involvement of local stakeholders can help create a positive image of CET and a sense of ownership throughout the community. Lolwana, Rabe and Morakane

(2018[10]) identify the lack of meaningful relationships with other education institutions and the labour market, and therefore the inability to help students develop effective learning pathways, as the number one weakness of the current CET system. Different stakeholders can provide insights on different types of needs:

- *Local labour market needs*: Local employers can give insights in the labour market needs in the local area. Firms can provide information on existing and planned vacancies, as well as the skill gaps observed among their current employees and job seekers more generally. Firms, and especially smaller ones, can also provide insights into entrepreneurial opportunities, and the skills needed to start a business. In this respect, firms from the informal sector should also be included in the consultation process. Strong ties with local employers could also be used to negotiate workplace-learning opportunities for CET students and graduates (e.g. internships). Similarly, SETAs are also well connected with local employers, and can assist CET institutions in engaging with them.
- *Social development needs:* NGOs often have close ties with the local communities, and can therefore provide valuable information on the needs of these communities. This information is not limited to labour market needs, but also relates to broader social development needs. Similarly, community leaders can have a good understanding of local needs. CET institutions can also set up partnerships with NGOs that already provide training opportunities for adults, to facilitate and encourage cooperation. Other government departments, such as social development, health and rural development can also provide useful insights into community needs.
- *Skills needs for further education:* The goal of the CET system is not only to prepare adults for the labour market, but also to facilitate the transition to TVET colleges and higher education institutions. Close relationships between CET institutions and TVET colleges and universities in the same area will allow for a better understanding of the skills needed to progress into these education institutions, and their training offer. Partnerships between CET institutions and other training providers can be set up to ensure that CET graduates get access to further education opportunities. Partnerships can also be formed to share resources (e.g. CET using the infrastructure of public or private TVET colleges for vocational programmes).

In addition, local government could also provide insights into the broad needs of communities, in addition to the needs identified in their Integrated Development Plans. Local governments generally have a good understanding of the problems in their area, and have close connections with key local stakeholders. At the same time, local governments often provide or finance training opportunities for adults, and close cooperation with them is therefore crucial to understand their training offer, but also to encourage them to finance training programmes in CET institutions.

Different strategies can be pursued to engage with local stakeholders. CET institutions can, for example, set up regular meetings with stakeholders, create a consultative body, appoint stakeholders to their governing board and/or enter into close partnership with certain key stakeholders. Box 5.2 describes how local community members are engaged in Canada and the United States. Sufficient capacity is needed in the CET system to set up and manage stakeholder engagements and partnerships.

Recommended action steps

provides some possible action steps that could be taken to engage local stakeholders in the CET system. For each action step, the most relevant stakeholders concerned are listed. The list of stakeholders is not exhaustive, and cooperation between different stakeholders is encouraged. The actions steps focus on the short- and medium-term, and a more ambitious action plan could be developed for the longer term in line with the vision for CET from the DHET's strategic documents.

Table 5.4. Action steps for engaging local stakeholders

Action steps and relevant stakeholders

Action steps	Main stakeholders
Train college and centre managers on how to engage with local stakeholders.	DHET, CET Colleges, CLCs
Identify key local stakeholders, potentially in partnership with the municipal government.	CET Colleges, CLCs, Municipal government
Invite identified key stakeholders for information session on their potential role in community education and training.	All
Engage with key stakeholders on a regular basis, to ensure that the course offering and content remains in line with local needs.	All
Include a set of key stakeholders in the governing boards (e.g. employers, NGOs).	All
Explore partnerships with (groups of) employers. Within these partnerships, the employers can co-design the training programmes, provided they offer job opportunities for graduates (internships or regular jobs) and/or training facilities (for the more technical programmes).	CET Colleges, CLCs, employers
Set up an information system to document stakeholder engagement. The evaluation of CLCs should take their performance in stakeholder engagement into account.	DHET, CET Colleges, CLCs

Note: DHET: Department for Higher Education and Training; CLC: Community Learning Centre; SETA: Sector Education and Training Authority; NGO: Non-Governmental Organisation.

5.5. Taking outcomes and feedback into account

In order to know if CET programmes are truly aligned with local needs, it is important to understand whether they had the desired impact on the participants and local stakeholders. These outcomes can be measured through satisfaction surveys, but also by tracking students after graduation. The current information system in CET is very weak, making it very difficult to measure the effectiveness of CET programmes and services (Lolwana, Rabe and Morakane, 2018[10]).

The main goal of vocational skills programmes in CET institutions is to improve the labour market prospects of participants by equipping them with skills that are in demand in the local labour market. For these programmes to be successful, they need to give graduates access to employment opportunities and provide a pool of well-trained candidates to local employers with recruitment needs. The positive outcomes can be measured through satisfaction surveys among participants and employers. Participants can be asked whether they were satisfied with the programme and whether it had a positive impact on their labour market outcomes. Similarly, employers who hired graduates can be asked about their satisfaction with the skill of the new recruits. Box 5.3 describes how Denmark collects and disseminates information from satisfaction surveys. An alternative and more objective way to measure outcomes is through the collection of information on employment rates of participants and rates of progress into further education. This information can be collected through tracer surveys, but also by setting up integrated information systems that link data on education enrolment and graduation with labour market information systems (e.g. unemployment insurance contributions).

Box 5.2. Involving community members in colleges in North America

Canada: Community members on governing boards of colleges

In Canada, most public colleges have community members on their governing boards. These boards are semi-autonomous, meaning that they must follow government policies and directives, but are free to implement them in a way that best suits their local community's realities. The community members include local employers, local community groups and local government. Governing board members generally act on a voluntary basis, i.e. without any compensation for their activities. The role of the business community is not limited to participation in governing boards, as local employers are often also members of committees that advise on course offering and curricula.

United States: Partnerships between community colleges and businesses

Many community colleges in the United States have formed partnerships with local employers to address labour market needs in their region. In many cases, employers from the same sector team up to co-operate with community colleges to develop and implement training programmes that address skill needs in their sector. In Sacramento, for example, community colleges and utilities have worked together to create programmes that develop skills for entry-level utility occupations in the region. In San Diego, local clean technology companies partnered with community colleges to design training programmes to prepare high-skilled workers for careers in the bio-fuels sector. The advantage for community colleges of forming a partnership with a group of employers rather than with one single employer is that the co-developed training programmes will not be employer-specific, allowing graduates to be more flexible and access a wider range of job opportunities in the labour market.

Source: Asian Development Bank (2015[11]), Brennan (2014[12]), Collaborative Economics (2015[13]).

In the same vein, the effectiveness of second chance programmes can be measured by looking at the share of graduates that continued to further education and the employment rate of those who do not pursue further education opportunities. For non-formal training and learning programmes, the outcomes are often less directly linked to the labour market or further education, and their impact can therefore mainly be measured through satisfaction surveys. The same holds for other services provided in CET institutions, such as career guidance and RPL support.

Training providers around the world are increasingly being assessed based on the outcomes of their students. In many OECD countries, quality assessment and certification of training providers takes into account the labour market outcomes and user satisfaction of training participants (OECD, 2019[14]). Chapter 6 provides more details on how to use the information on outcomes for quality assurance.

Box 5.3. *Vis Kvalitet*: Denmark's tool for measuring training quality

The Danish Ministry of Education introduced a nationwide online tool for measuring the quality of vocational education and training. The purpose of the tool is to measure the satisfaction of participants, as well as their learning outcomes, but also the satisfaction of enterprises whose employees have participated in vocational training. It is a flexible tool that offers the possibility of inserting optional questions at regional and local levels to measure other aspects of interest to parties such as providers and regional councils. The use of the tool is compulsory for training providers.

Participants are asked questions on the usefulness of training, but also the satisfaction with teachers and the form and content teaching. Certain questions directly ask about the usefulness of training for employment opportunities. The unemployed are asked whether training helped them access better opportunities to find a job. Questions for the employed refer to the use of the newly acquired skills in the workplace and to whether or not the training enabled them to carry out new tasks in their current job.

The data are shared with the broad public on a website (www.viskvalitet.dk) to help students and adults make informed education and training choices. This also provides an incentive to training providers to invest in the quality of their programmes. Ratings are made available as soon as a minimum number of answers have been received.

Source: Cedefop (2011[15]); Bolvig, Kiil and Kristensen (2015[16]); Zibrowius (2018[17]).

Recommended action steps

Table 5.5 provides some possible action steps that could be taken to collect feedback and information on outcomes from CET students. For each action step, the most relevant stakeholders concerned are listed. The list of stakeholders is not exhaustive, and cooperation between different stakeholders is encouraged. The actions steps focus on the short- and medium-term, and a more ambitious action plan could be developed for the longer term in line with the vision for CET from the DHET's strategic documents.

Table 5.5. Action steps for collection information on students' satisfaction and outcomes

Action steps and relevant stakeholders

Action steps	Main stakeholders
Develop standardised satisfaction surveys (online and paper versions). CET institutions should be able to add questions if desired.	DHET
Administer the survey with students during and at the end of the training programmes, but also with participants in career guidance sessions and employers hiring CET graduates.	CLCs, employers
Set up an information system to bring together the survey results. This will allow CET institutions to get a synthesised view of the satisfaction of their students, and evaluate their performance.	DHET, CET Colleges, CLCs
Develop tracer studies that can be administered among recent graduates.	DHET, TVET colleges, Universities
Carefully register all students, including contact details. This could be used for tracing surveys or for linking the CET database to other databases (e.g. social security, unemployment insurance).	CLCs

Note: DHET: Department for Higher Education and Training; CLC: Community Learning Centre; SETA: Sector Education and Training Authority; TVET: Technical and Vocational Education and Training.

Note

[1] Information on vacancies is one of the components used by the DHET to calculate the occupations in high demand (Reddy et al., 2017[18]).

References

Asian Development Bank (2015), *The role of community colleges in skills development: Lessons from the Canadian experience for developing Asia*, Asian Development Bank, https://www.adb.org/sites/default/files/publication/177058/role-community-colleges-skills-development.pdf (accessed on 4 June 2018). [11]

Bolvig, I., A. Kiil and N. Kristensen (2015), *Videreudvikling af Vis Kvalitet*, Kora, Kopenhagen. [16]

Brennan, P. (2014), "Raising the quality and image of TVET: Lower-level training or motor for inclusive and sustainable growth?", *PROSPECTS*, Vol. 44/2, pp. 183-195, http://dx.doi.org/10.1007/s11125-014-9312-3. [12]

Cedefop (2011), "Assuring quality in vocational education and training: The role of accrediting VET providers", *Cedefop Reference series*, No. 90, Cedefop. [15]

Collaborative Economics (2015), *Next Generation Industry Engagement: Toward a Shared Investment Approach to High-Demand Workforce Training*, The Morgan Family Foundation, http://doingwhatmatters.cccco.edu/portals/6/docs/SW/MorganProfiles_2015.pdf (accessed on 4 June 2018). [13]

Dyer, C. and P. Rose (2005), "Decentralisation for educational development? An editorial introduction", *Compare: A Journal of Comparative and International Education*, Vol. 35/2, pp. 105-113, http://dx.doi.org/10.1080/03057920500129809. [3]

Lolwana, P., E. Rabe and M. Morakane (2018), "Who accesses adult education and where do they progress to? An exploratory tracer study in community education and training", *LMIP reports*, No. 37, Labour Market Intelligence Parternship, http://www.lmip.org.za/document/who-accesses-adult-education-and-where-do-they-progress-exploratory-tracer-study-community (accessed on 7 November 2018). [10]

OECD (2019), *Getting Skills Right: Future-Ready Adult Learning Systems*, Getting Skills Right, OECD Publishing, Paris, https://dx.doi.org/10.1787/9789264311756-en. [14]

OECD (2018), *The Future of Education and Skills: Education 2030*, OECD, Paris, https://www.oecd.org/education/2030/E2030%20Position%20Paper%20(05.04.2018).pdf (accessed on 7 August 2018). [5]

OECD (2017), *Getting Skills Right: South Africa*, Getting Skills Right, OECD Publishing, Paris, http://dx.doi.org/10.1787/9789264278745-en. [9]

OECD (2016), *Getting Skills Right: Assessing and Anticipating Changing Skill Needs*, Getting Skills Right, OECD Publishing, Paris, http://dx.doi.org/10.1787/9789264252073-en. [8]

OECD (2016), *Job Creation and Local Economic Development 2016*, OECD Publishing, Paris, http://dx.doi.org/10.1787/9789264261976-en. [7]

OECD (2014), *Skills beyond School: Synthesis Report*, OECD Reviews of Vocational Education and Training, OECD Publishing, Paris, http://dx.doi.org/10.1787/9789264214682-en. [6]

OECD (2013), *PISA 2012 Results: What Makes Schools Successful (Volume IV): Resources, Policies and Practices*, PISA, OECD Publishing, Paris, http://dx.doi.org/10.1787/9789264201156-en. [2]

Reddy, V. et al. (2017), *Occupations in High Demand in South Africa - A Technical Report*, LMIP. [18]

Unesco (2016), *Community-based lifelong learning and adult education: Situations of community learning centres in 7 Asian countries*, Unesco, Bangkok. [1]

Unesco (2014), *Education microplanning toolkit: introductory module*, Asia and Pacific Regional Bureau for Education, Bangkok, http://www.unesco.org/open-access/terms-use-ccbysa-en (accessed on 7 August 2018). [4]

Zibrowius, M. (2018), *Promoting Social Partnership in Employee Training: EU Social Partners' Project on Employee Training - Country Report Denmark*, German Economic Institute, Cologne, https://www.etuc.org/sites/default/files/publication/file/2018-06/DK_Country%20report%20Denmark_final.pdf (accessed on 10 July 2018). [17]

Chapter 6. Ensuring quality in Community Education and Training institutions

The CET system faces many challenges in light of its foreseen expansion and diversification. This chapter looks at key quality challenges in the CET system, focusing on addressing issues around an inadequately prepared and qualified teaching workforce, and insufficient quality assurance mechanisms. These two aspects are crucial for improving the quality and impact of the CET system.

6.1. Background

High quality of education is important to ensure that adults are effectively equipped to participate in the society at large and in the labour market, capable to learn at a higher level, and prepared to subsequently engage in future learning activities to update their knowledge and skills. Quality is often a challenge in education and training, because it has many different aspects and is difficult to assess (OECD, 2014[1]; OECD, 2013[2]). This is particularly challenging in the area of adult learning, as it is encompasses a large variety of programmes delivered by many different providers (OECD, 2019[3]).

The objectives of education and training programmes for adults are very diverse, and therefore not all programmes will have to adhere to the same quality criteria. High-quality programmes and institutions are designed to meet the needs of their students and give them the tools to complete the programme and to transition into the next steps (e.g. a good job, further education opportunities, and sustainable livelihoods). This means that the programmes need to be adapted to the specific needs of adult learners - both in terms of learning methods and flexible schedules that allow combining education with work and family responsibilities (see Chapter 3). When large numbers of students fail to complete a programme or when they do not transition into further education and training, this signals quality issues.

Quality assurance mechanisms are an essential part of any education and training system. Well-designed evaluation and assessment activities are expected to ensure that: i) each student is provided with high-quality and relevant education; ii) the overall education system is contributing to the social and economic development of the country; and iii) each education agent is performing at their best to deliver efficient education services (OECD, 2013[2]). Quality assurance systems come from different starting points, depending on the organisation of the network of providers (for example their ownership and management), the funding and accountability mechanisms in place, and the way the qualifications and programmes are regulated.

The adult learning opportunities in the CET system in South Africa are extensive, but face multiple quality challenges, including high dropout rates, inadequate infrastructure, courses that do not correspond to the specific needs and preferences of adult learners and an inadequately prepared and qualified workforce as well as insufficient quality assurance mechanisms. Many of these challenges are inter-connected: for example, unless programmes are adapted to the needs of adults, outcomes will remain poor. South Africa's National Improvement Plan for teaching and learning for Community Education and Training (see Annex A) recognises underperformance by the sector. With the new expansion plans, the CET system will broaden its offer to more students – aiming to reach 1 million by 2030 – and a larger diversity of programmes. This significant expansion in a relatively short period of time needs to be handled carefully to minimise the risk of quality issues. The next sections look at two areas that are essential to improve the quality of the CET system: ensuring that CET staff are adequately prepared and qualified, and building a quality framework and implementing appropriate assurance mechanisms.

6.2. Tackling challenges in preparing and qualifying CET lecturers and leaders

Since teachers are the most important resource in education institutions, it is essential to focus on them to improve education quality. The demands on teachers for adults are usually very complex, and represent true challenges to the profession (OECD, 2005[4]). The CET sector will face two separate challenges: i) the qualification and professional development of the existing workforce, and ii) recruitment of new teachers, leaders and support staff. Given the scale of the planned expansion, a lot of emphasis will be on initial teacher training, attracting new people to the profession and giving them the right set of skills, appropriate for teaching adults. Importantly, the right conditions need to be in place to make the profession attractive.

Building a workforce that is adequately prepared and qualified

The sector suffers from a lack of attractiveness due to poor working conditions

Around 16 000 lecturers are employed in the CET system (Parliamentary Monitoring Group, 2018[5]). The Department of Higher Education and Training's (DHET) 2013 White Paper articulates many weaknesses. The majority of lecturers in CET programmes are part-time contract workers with no tenure. The sector does not have a core of permanent adult lecturers, and conditions are not uniform between provinces. This severely affects long-term planning and leaves little room for career and learning pathway development for lecturers (Department of Higher Education and Training, 2013[6]). According to the South African ABET Educators Union (SAAEU), challenges include low pay and non-payment of salaries, non-recognition of Adult Education and Training (AET) diplomas, bullying by centre managers, as well as teachers having two jobs ('double-parking') (Parliamentary Monitoring Group, 2017[7]).

Many teachers are not adequately prepared

Initial teacher education and teaching qualifications represent the entry point into the profession, and the way these qualifications are organised plays a key role in determining both the quality and the quantity of teachers (OECD, 2005[4]).

According to the DHET's guidelines, teachers in the sector must have specialised knowledge of pedagogical approaches that are relevant to adults, and work with curriculum differentiation to address individual learning needs (Department of Higher Education and Training, 2015[8]). Nevertheless, many teachers do not have the pedagogical tools to teach adults. Educators in the CET system hold a variety of qualifications, including grade 12 school-leaving certificates, SETA-accredited ABET Level 4 and ABET Level 5 certificates, as well as diplomas, degrees and post-graduate degrees. Recent reports say that between 30-40% of CET staff are under-qualified or not qualified at all, particularly in rural areas (Parliamentary Monitoring Group, 2018[5]). Recent numbers reported by the DHET, which show that 37.5% of lectures in CET do not have the minimum requirement for employment in education (i.e. Matric + 3 years, REQV 13), confirm this (see Figure 6.1). This share reaches more than 45% in the KwaZulu-Natal and Northern Cape provinces. These under-qualified teachers are generally not prepared for their roles (Department of Higher Education and Training, 2015[8]). The DHET did not have a strategy to deal with the phenomenon of the appointment of unqualified teachers and there were no measures to track and monitor the extent of unqualified educators and correct the situation. Recently, unqualified teachers were given a set period to become qualified (Parliamentary Monitoring Group, 2017[7]).

This situation creates the need for relevant qualification programmes for adult educators and CET lecturers (which focus on pedagogical methods for adults), but also for mechanisms to ensure that educators and lecturers in these institutions actually hold the required qualifications. There are on-going plans to change the qualification programmes for lecturers in the system, setting minimum standards for these qualifications

(Department of Higher Education and Training, 2015[8]). Universities and TVET colleges are supposed to contribute to developing the capacity to train adult educators (Department of Higher Education and Training, 2015[9]). By making initial teaching programme flexible, for example with distance learning, entering the CET teaching body could be made more attractive for new recruits. It is also very important that teachers have access to continuing professional development, not only to ensure that skills of teachers remain up-to-date but also to keep teachers motivated (Musset, 2010[10]).

Figure 6.1. Many CET lecturers do not have the required qualifications

% of CET lectures at different REQV qualification levels (2017)

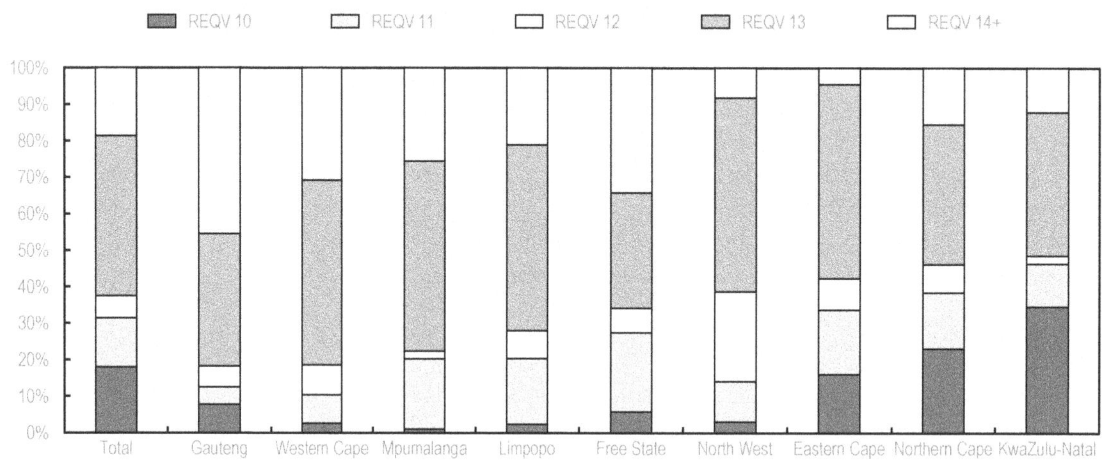

Note: The different lecturer qualification are presented on the Relative Education Qualification Value (REQV) scale. REQV 10 corresponds to Matric level qualification, and REQV (10+x) levels correspond roughly to Matric + x years of further education. See Republic of South Africa (2000[11]) for more details on the REQV scale. Provinces are ranked by the share of teachers with a qualification level below REQV 13.
Source: Data provided by the Department for Higher Education and Training.

As the CET system will deliver a wide range of programmes, it would make sense to develop different qualifications associated with different types of programmes, rather than to try to develop one set of qualifications suited for all lecturers. De facto, this means that there will need to be teachers in CET institutions to teach literacy and numeracy, as well as vocational skills to adults (not the same teachers need to handle both of these). Mismatch of subjects being taught and lecturer qualifications might increase (Parliamentary Monitoring Group, 2018[5]). In practice, the shifting from academic programmes to more skill-focus ones has been slowed down by the fact that most lecturers were school teachers, not prepared to teach the new subjects nor to work with adults. To secure an adequate teaching workforce in the institutions, one option could be to create closer ties between the CET institutions and the other types of education and training institutions to share teaching staff across different sites.

Enforcing that only qualified lecturers can be appointed could – at this point – have strongly negative impacts, and lead to some education institutions shutting down. The implementation of teaching qualifications for all teachers in CET can be gradual, and based on a combination of RPL (Recognition of Prior Learning) mechanisms for those who have the right set of skills but are not qualified as teachers, and professional development courses for those who have skill gaps, leading to teaching qualifications. A system of professional development for teachers already exists under the South African Council for Educators (SACE), which lies with the Department of Basic Education. SACE registers all educators and manages a system of professional development called Continuing Professional Teacher Development (CPTD). Teachers have a CPTD accounts that tracks the professional development activities they participated in (SACE, 2019[12]).

Vocational lecturers face specific challenges

In the case of vocational subjects, it is important that teachers have relevant experience in their field (OECD, 2010[13]; 2014[11]). It provides lecturers with a context for their teaching, and increases their confidence in teaching for their occupation. In line with South Africa's proposed reforms for TVET colleges (Department of Higher Education and Training, 2012[14]), international experience suggests that vocational lecturers and teachers in all institutions, including the CET system, should be encouraged to spend time at the workplace. For example, in Finland, the Telkkä programme allowed teachers to spend two months on-the-job and brought a wide range of benefits to teachers (Box 6.1). One benefit of teacher-internships is that teachers become more familiar with current workplace requirements.

Box 6.1. Teacher-worker pairing: co-operation between VET and employers in Finland

The Telkkä programme in Finland was based on close co-operation between teachers and workplace trainers. It aimed to improve the ability of VET to respond to the needs of working life. The programme included a two-month on-the-job period for teachers, during which teacher-worker pairs were formed. This offered an opportunity for teachers to update their professional skills and for workers who also work as workplace trainers to improve their pedagogical skills. The training period was preceded by a seminar and planning (to clarify goals and expectations) and followed by feedback from teachers and workers and dissemination to the broader community. Teachers reported a wide range of benefits, such as increased familiarity with recent work practices and requirements and the equipment used, easy access to firms for study visits, the contacts necessary to invite people from industry to give lectures at their VET institutions, increased confidence, respect from students and motivation. The training period also allowed teachers and workers to discuss issues related to workplace training for students and improve training plans and assessment methods. Participants improve their skills and self-esteem, and disseminate knowledge to other colleagues. This exercise has been evaluated by the Economic Information Office in Finland as one of the best ways of developing teachers' professionalism.

Source: Cort, Härkönen and Volmari (2004[15]).

Today, vocational lecturers in TVET colleges in South Africa already face multiple challenges. With the development of the TVET sector, the majority of new lecturers came from a general education background rather than a vocational one, and often have either diploma or degree-level qualifications. With the introduction of the NCV, most of them felt inadequately qualified (Buthelezi, 2018[16]). Field, Musset and Álvarez-Galván (2014[17]) found that at least 25% of TVET lecturers currently lack teaching qualifications and more than half have no industry experience. Almost half of the teaching staff have short-term contracts giving them little incentive to make longer-term investments in skills and qualifications. It is likely that the vocational lecturers in the CET system will face similar issues. There are interesting alternative professional development models that are in place in the TVET sector, by which lecturers can update their lecturing qualification using a mix of distance and contact sessions, either on week days or Saturdays (DHET, 2019[18]). Under this model, put in place in the KwaZulu-Natal province, training programmes are developed to train the trainers, and shared training needs between different colleges are identified. The objective is to increase the share of lecturers that are qualified, and improve their skills, while also supporting retention. At the national level, the DHET has also launched an innovative approach through the TVET Lecturer Support System for those already in service, through videos and activities, supported by college-based facilitators (DHET, 2018[19]).

Flexible and alternative pathways to enter the lecturing workforce

When recruiting lecturers, education systems and institutions have to compete with other labour market opportunities. This is particularly the case when systems are unable to offer competitive salaries. In the case of vocational lecturers, the competition can be particularly fierce with jobs in industry.

Alternative and quicker pathways into the teaching profession can help alleviate teacher shortages, while also act as an incentive to bring capable people with previous experience in other fields into the teacher workforce. Programmes that provide alternative pathways rely on teacher candidates' previous education and work experience. Experience from countries shows that these programmes can be short and consist mainly of practical training (Musset, 2010[10]). The '*Teach for America*' alternative certification programme, created in 1990, recruits and trains university graduates and professionals for a two-year teaching assignments in disadvantaged public schools. After a five-week summer course, participants start teaching while receiving on-going professional development. In despite of criticisms about their lack of adequate preparation, their attrition rate is lower than that of traditional teacher education programmes graduates, and these teachers are more effective than other beginner teachers, especially in mathematics and science (Xu, Hannaway and Taylor, 2007[20]).

Recruiting professionals as lecturers can be particularly helpful in ensuring that vocational teachers have up-to-date technical skills. Lecturers who have worked in industry bring with them not only their practical knowledge but also their network of contacts and personal relationships with their previous colleagues. These networks can be shared, and they powerfully support co-operation between vocational schools and industry, including the arrangement of work-based learning opportunities for students (OECD, 2010[13]).

The DHET should also consider promoting arrangements such as part-time teaching, which could facilitate the entry of workers from industry into the profession. Typically, such arrangements require pedagogical training, but it is unrealistic and undesirable to impose the same demands on these part-time teachers as on full-time teaching staff. For example in South Carolina (United States), individuals with relevant work experience in some fields (for example in welding, cosmetology and culinary arts) can enter the teaching profession through the state's Career and Technical Education work-based certification and training programme. It provides them with training in methods of teaching, classroom and laboratory management, curriculum and assessment, delivered in a block of a couple of days over the summer and on a few weekend days during the school year (South Carolina Department of Education, 2018[21]). For a successful implementation, the DHET needs to make sure that the pathways into teaching are well known and appealing.

Strengthening the leadership of institutions

Responsibilities of leaders are wide and broadening

Across countries, school leaders often enter their roles with limited preparation (OECD, 2010[13]; 2014[1]). South Africa is no exception. Historically, limited efforts were made in CET institutions and TVET colleges to support and prepare college directors to carry out their duties. There have been major leadership challenges, and issues of mismanagement. In the case of TVET colleges for example, a number of institutions have been taken temporarily under the authority of central administration in order to address mismanagement, with college leaders replaced by interim leaders appointed for limited periods, (Field, Musset and Álvarez-Galván, 2014[17]).

With the reform and the broadening of the scope of the CET system, the responsibilities of the CET institutions are multiple, and very ambitious. Leaders of CET institutions need to engage in both short and long-term planning, develop strong relationships with local employers, government officials, and other stakeholders, and be familiar with enrolment trends, programme developments, and a wide range of administrative details. The draft policy guidelines state that the CET institutions must (among other things) (Department of Higher Education and Training, 2016[22]):

- Prepare and administer high quality theoretical and practical assessment tasks for internal continuous assessments;
- Undertake revision of units of learning to improve student performance where deficiencies and gaps are evident;
- Monitor the quality of curriculum delivery;
- Collect student data that allows to build a comprehensive sociological profile of each student including, but not limited to, entry-level education attainment, age, gender, disability, geography and race;
- Prepare well-formulated and well-paced lessons;
- Prepare learning support materials that support the intended curriculum delivery approach;
- Source additional learning materials to support weaker students and extend to more capable students.

These are all very worthy and ambitious objectives, but their implementation will require specific training for both lecturers and school leaders. This also gives a lot of responsibilities to leaders in terms of the selection and professional development of lecturers.

Effective school leadership is key to education quality

In many countries, including in South Africa, schools leaders have ever-greater responsibilities, with decentralization and greater school autonomy. Across countries, in general education, but to a lesser extent also in vocational and in adult education, there has been increasing recognition that effective leadership is vital in developing the skills of classroom teachers, and attention to leadership can therefore represent an important means of driving up the quality of teaching and learning (Pont, Nusche and Moorman, 2008[23]). Leadership may be even more important in institutions that have a diverse teaching workforce, including different occupational skills, and different mixes of industry experience and pedagogical qualifications and skills (Field, Musset and Álvarez-Galván, 2014[17]). Institutions can also face challenges in securing an appropriate supply of non-teaching administrative support staff.

Strong leaders need well-defined roles and must be accountable. Opportunities for career progression for lecturers into leadership roles can also contribute to making the teaching profession more attractive for potential lecturers. The requirements on school leaders need to be linked to a shared vision of effective schooling. School leaders play a pivotal role in encouraging lecturers to pursue collaborative learning within and across schools. This is especially important in a context in which lecturers may not receive a lot of professional development.

There is a continuing trend in OECD countries towards giving education institutions, either through their professional staff or school boards, discretion in hiring lecturers and (to a lesser extent) firing them. This also implies providing the resources for schools to act. However, a high degree of self-management may not be a solution for school systems where capacity and leadership are still to be developed. Providing administrative arrangements that support schools is now a key issue across OECD countries (OECD, 2010[24]).

Many countries have recently developed demanding programmes for the development of education institution leaders

Since the mid-1990s, training and development for school leaders, in particular for secondary education, have been introduced in many OECD countries. Training arrangements include i) preservice or preparatory training to take up the position; ii) induction training for those who have recently taken up the position; and iii) in-service training provided to practising school leaders. Countries like England, Finland, Northern Ireland, Israel and Slovenia provide leadership development training at all steps in a school leader's career. Chile, Ireland, the Netherlands and Norway have in-service education programmes. The courses offered to actual or prospective college leaders may vary from short certificate courses to post-graduate or PhD Programmes. Training may also vary depending on the responsibilities of school leaders, such as the extent of school or college control over matters like staffing and budgets (Pont, Nusche and Moorman, 2008[23]).

Given the current plans to strengthen the CET system, and the very wide responsibilities that will be attributed the college and centre managers, an opportunity exists to build quality through a relatively small number of highly effective CET institution leaders. Such leaders need to be able to support the professional development of individual lecturers, develop new skills programmes in partnership with SETAs and local authorities, which are adapted to local needs, and build partnerships with other education and training providers. These are substantial demands, requiring systematic professional development, and the training programmes for such leaders should be aligned with what is asked from them. To prepare the leaders who will run these institutions is as important as providing the infrastructure for the programmes.

Recommended action steps

Table 6.1 provides some possible action steps that could be taken to improve the quality of the workforce in the CET system, including lecturers and institution leaders. For each action step, the most relevant stakeholders concerned are listed. The list of stakeholders is not exhaustive, and cooperation between different stakeholders is encouraged. The actions steps focus on the short- and medium-term, and a more ambitious action plan could be developed for the longer term in line with the vision for CET from the DHET's strategic documents.

Table 6.1. Action steps for quality of the CET workforce

Action steps and relevant stakeholders

Action steps	Main stakeholders
Make sure that lecturers in the CET system are qualified, by gradually implementing training policies using professional development and RPL mechanisms that give opportunities to obtain the adequate qualifications to those already lecturing.	DHET, CET Colleges, CLC, TVET colleges, universities
Ensure that lecturers have access to on-going professional development to address their skill gaps and progress to becoming fully qualified.	DHET, DBE
Consider developing alternative and flexible pathways into the lecturing profession, especially in the case of shortages, for vocational subjects.	DHET, TVET colleges, universities, SETAs
Facilitate the entry of skilled professionals into the workforce of CET institutions for specific subjects through shortened pedagogical preparation. Encourage part-time working among vocational lecturers.	DHET
Allow for flexible work arrangements, so that lecturers can simultaneous work in different institutions.	DHET, DBE, TVET colleges, Universities
Give more security and working hours to lecturers to make teaching in CET more attractive, and assess the core working conditions of CET lecturers to see what the challenges are regarding the lack of attractiveness of the profession (e.g. timely payment of wages).	DHET, DBE
Carefully select and prepare the leaders of CET institutions, taking into account the characteristics of the institutions and their responsibilities.	DHET, CET Colleges
Ensure that CET institutions have enough non-lecturing support staff, and make sure that adequate mechanisms for their selection and preparation are in place	DHET

Note: DHET: Department for Higher Education and Training; DBE: Department for Basic Education; TVET: Technical and Vocational Education and Training; CLC: Community Learning Centre.

6.3. Building a quality framework and strengthening quality assurance mechanisms

Quality assurance is a necessary part of an efficient and effective adult learning system. Effective evaluation and assessment of learners, lecturers and CET institutions depend on a shared understanding of quality and what counts as good outcomes. Quality assurance arrangements are fundamental to ensure that programmes and qualifications are consistent throughout a system. Funding arrangements can also be designed with quality standards in mind, by linking them to certain desirable outcomes. In the absence of policies to ensure quality, adult programmes can exacerbate existing economic and social inequalities, channelling often low skilled and financially vulnerable students into low quality programmes that do not lead to good outcomes (in terms of learning experience and skills, but also labour market outcomes). The following sections focus on different policies that could help building and implementing a quality framework.

Current quality assurance arrangements for CET fall short

The decision to create a National Qualification Framework (NQF) in 1995 aimed to build new forms of equality across apartheid's differences, not only between fields of education and training, but across other socio-economic divisions that they reinforced. However, in its implementation, it failed to become hegemonic (Lugg, 2009[25]). The NQF did not manage to create a unified quality assurance system, as it consists of three Quality Councils (the Council for Higher Education, the Quality Council for Trades and Occupations, and the Council for General and Further Education and Training) and an oversight body (SAQA). This particular design of the framework reflects the deep differences between parts of the education and training system (Walters and Isaacs, 2014[26]). Lugg (2009[25]) argues that struggles over the NQF have been simultaneously struggles over the nature of the state, the economy, education institutions and the relationships between them; struggles articulating with differing and often contradictory globalised discourses, but played out within local histories and political contexts.

Given that CET institutions will be providing a wide range of education and training programmes, they will fall under the responsibility of different quality councils. On the one hand, quality assurance of the vocational programmes will be the responsibility of the Quality Council for Trades and Occupations (QCTO), which was created to bring together the quality assurance role undertaken by the SETAs. However, specific individual training programmes continue to be under the responsibilities of SETAs, and often the division of responsibilities is unclear. On the other hand, general academic qualifications (GETC:ABET and National Senior Certificate Amended) are under the responsibility of Umalusi. When institutions have to quality-assure qualifications with two or more different agencies that use different methodologies, the transaction costs are higher for the institutions.

Developing a quality framework through consultation with stakeholders

A good quality framework and system needs to be simple and easily understandable by all stakeholders. An important step in this direction is a national reflection, involving all the stakeholders, to reach a common understanding and a consensus about what constitutes quality in CET in South Africa, and to agree on a framework to assess CET outcomes and the quality of institutions. The development of a quality framework can empower lecturers and institution leaders, and serve as the basis for self-evaluation. In the current context, discussions about a quality framework can form part of a broader discussion on what should be the mandate and the shape of the CET system.

At the outset, a quality framework can allow to articulate coherently the different components of evaluation and assessment. Achieving proper articulation between the different evaluation components (e.g. school evaluation and lecturer appraisal) and warranting that the several elements within an evaluation component are sufficiently linked (e.g. teaching standards and teacher appraisal; external school evaluation and school self-evaluation) is very important. The results of the school evaluation (both self-evaluation and external) and teacher appraisal must be linked to initial teacher education and professional development strategies (OECD, 2013[2]).

Creating an effective evaluation and assessment framework requires capacity development at all levels of the education system. For example, lecturers may need training in the use of formative assessment (as mentioned in Chapter 4), CET staff may need to upgrade their skills in managing data, and institutions managers – who often focus mainly on administrative tasks – may need to reinforce their leadership skills. In addition, a centralised effort may be needed to develop a knowledge base, tools and guidelines to assist evaluation and assessment activities.

Implementing accreditation processes to clarify quality standards for institutions

In countries with a large public provision of adult learning, there generally are public institutions in charge of quality control and evaluation. Quality assurance agencies have the responsibility to regulate institutions and assure that the services they provide is of high quality and consistent throughout their jurisdiction. Their responsibilities can also include co-ordination within government, as well as between government and a wide range of nongovernment actors such as employers, trade unions, private and public educational institutions, and community groups (OECD, 2003). Many countries make accreditation a requirement for any institutions to award particular qualifications and to be eligible for public funding. Institutional accreditation can be a valuable complement to other policies such as institutional inspections (Eichhorst et al., 2012[27]).

Accreditation systems are designed to establish clear quality standards for education and training providers and programmes. Institutions are evaluated in relation to a set of established quality standards that the participating institution has agreed to sustain in exchange for becoming accredited (those quality standards are part of the framework that is agreed between stakeholders as mentioned before). Teams of reviewers carry out the accreditation process, visiting an institution, determining the extent to which the standards are met, and publicly announcing their findings (Council for Higher Education Accreditation, 2010[28]). An interesting accreditation process is used by the South African Council for Educators (SACE): To ensure that educators have access to high-quality continuing training opportunities, SACE approves high-quality and credible training providers based on specific quality criteria, endorses good and relevant training programmes and allocates professional development points to these activities (SACE, 2019[12]).

However, accreditation systems are difficult to establish, and even more so when there are many entrenched institutions that have little to gain from such new procedures. While accreditation is far from a panacea, it can establish an important quality baseline and support efforts to increase institutional accountability. For South Africa, the shift in responsibility for adult learning centres from provincial education departments to the DHET can help to ensure consistency in the qualifications and the programmes, and institutional accreditation could help ensure minimum standards are met. This is especially important in the CET context, in which institutions with very different levels of quality are being put under the same umbrella. For accreditation to work as a guarantor of quality, it has to be mandatory, not voluntary, and it needs to be part of a broader set of accountability policies that aim to guide institutional behaviour (McCarthy and Musset, 2016[29]). By relying on a framework developed in consensus with stakeholders as mentioned before and using it to set standards for which to conduct reviews and institution inspections, accreditation can create a sense of shared ownership in the quality assurance processes. It can also build the trust of students, employers, and policymakers in particular centres and programmes by establishing clear and consistent standards (Council for Higher Education Accreditation, 2010[28]).

Institution self-evaluation, against the set quality framework, could be introduced as an intermediate step before moving towards a system of mandatory accreditation. Providing tools to practitioners on how to measure their performance against the standards agreed in the quality framework can help build awareness around quality issues. It helps institutions examine their own practices through a critical lens and identify strengths and weakness. Self-evaluation can help to empower lecturers and educational leaders, not as an end in itself, but rather as a key step in the path to establishing a culture of continuous improvement in institutions (OECD, 2013[2]). When implementing a system that relies on quality standards, it is of crucial importance that education and training providers have a clear understanding of these standards. In Japan, workshops are organised to get training providers acquainted with quality guidelines (see Box 6.2)

In the case of South Africa, the accreditation process could have two different levels. First, a mandatory accreditation process can establish minimum requirements institutions need to comply with if they wish to receive public funding. Given the cost and time associated with review processes, these requirements would need to be implemented gradually. Second, a voluntary process can be made available for institutions that wish to see where and how they could improve (self-evaluation). The introduction of standards and learner assessment can help identify and support those CET institutions lagging behind.

Box 6.2. Implementing quality assurance guidelines for private training providers in Japan

In Japan, guidelines for vocational training services at private providers were developed in 2011 by the Ministry of Health, Labour and Welfare. The guidelines present specific measures to improve the quality of vocational training services and management of private providers based on an international quality standard. From 2018 onwards, training providers who comply with the quality assurance guidelines are being certified. Compliance is assessed based on documents submitted by the training providers and on-site visits.

Workshops are organised for training providers to get familiar with and better understand the quality assurance guidelines. The workshops aim to develop knowledge and skills required to conduct vocational training using a cycle of planning, doing, checking and acting:

- Plan: Identifying training needs and setting curricula and courses
- Do: Conducting training efficiently
- Check: Evaluating and auditing training
- Act: Reviewing and improving training

The government is considering making participation in workshops compulsory for training providers that want to offer publicly funded training programmes.

Source: OECD (OECD, 2019[3]), JEED (2018[30]).

Monitoring the system to inform the organisation of the network

Within the establishment of an accreditation system, there could be a stocktaking exercise of the entire CET system. This would allow to identify gaps and duplications in the provision, and to adapt it to the needs. This should involve an in-depth evaluation of the network's strengths and weaknesses, which should be done in addition to the mechanisms already in place. For the time being, the DHET has annual reports from the CET colleges as part of the monitoring function. In addition to this, CET Colleges submit annual diagnostic reports and an annual Education Management Information System survey is done as well (Parliamentary Monitoring Group, 2018[5]). This in-depth evaluation of strengths and weaknesses could allow differentiating training provision based on the strength of each Community Learning Centre, and inform the creation of the CET colleges that oversee the activities of the Community Learning Centres. For example, centres with strong ties with SETAs and/or with local employers can focus on delivering the vocational programmes, while centres with a good track record in literacy and numeracy can focus on such programmes. Such an exercise requires good data. South Africa has meaningful experience in consolidating a fragmented system into a handful of well-managed institutions, with the recent reform of the TVET college sector (Field, Musset and Álvarez-Galván, 2014[17]).

Building a good data collection and monitoring system

There are very ambitious plans to build a monitoring system based on data

Data allows to understand the needs of the students and the patterns in participation and completion, and to identify quality issues in the system. The Plan on Teaching and Learning for CET (Department of Higher Education and Training, 2017[31]) states that CET institutions should have a tool for evaluation of the quality of teaching. The DHET is considering the development of a performance management review to ensure that there is proper oversight of teaching and learning quality to give early warnings if intervention is needed (Parliamentary Monitoring Group, 2018[5]). According to DHET guidelines, it is the responsibility of the CET College management to set up a robust learner assessment regime which monitors the performance of lecturers and of the students (Department of Higher Education and Training, 2016[32]). The guidelines foresee that at the end of each programme, the throughput and completion rates, as well as the pass rates per subject, will be monitored and subjected to further analysis to determine whether the students' good or poor performance can be attributed to the lecturers. The performance trends must be monitored over time to determine whether the system's performance is improving, inconsistent or deteriorating. Based on the results, additional support could be directed either to the lecturers, through continuing professional development, or to the students. This would also allow accounting for the public resources invested in each college. This is a praiseworthy but also very ambitious goal, and it is not sure that this is feasible in the short or medium term given current capacity constraints.

In practice, this will require that all institutions collect and report the right data elements, including enrolments, retention, dropouts, course completion, and graduation rates, and in a reliable way. Building a data infrastructure to support an outcomes-driven system is not easy. Giving education institutions the responsibility for data collection and analysis generally has two problems. First, these institutions will rarely have the capacity to do this adequately, unless they receive sufficient support. Second, even if they do it well, it will generally not be done consistently across institutions, and consistency is necessary for comparative institutional analysis. Therefore, there are strong arguments for central control of data collection and analysis, while encouraging individual institutions to make full use of the data. Implementing such a data system will require extensive collaboration across national education, labour, and statistical agencies to connect education and employment data from around the country. The more the Department can facilitate accurate data collection through development of technology, technical assistance and training, the more likely it is to get accurate data from the CET institutions (see Chapter 4).

Assessment of student performance can be seen as a tool to reveal best practices and to encourage school improvement. However, "raw" school performance measures reflect not only the varying performance of teachers and schools, but also the socio-economic background of students. Accountability measures should therefore draw on a broad range of assessment information to make judgements about performance. Evaluation in this area is a particularly challenging task, since the goals of community education and training are more varied and idiosyncratic than those of conventional education or employment-focused training programmes. In addition, the DHET also need to ensure that the institutions are collecting data on students' background.

Good data can help link funding to outcomes

As mentioned in Chapter 5, collecting information on outcomes and satisfaction is important to ensure that the training and services delivered in the CET system correspond to the need of the community members and are of high quality. Outcome-based funding is one way in which education institutions can be encouraged to invest in quality. The principle is that institutions that perform well on certain desirable outcomes can be eligible for public funding, in a targeted and conditional way. As a principle of accountability, quality assurance of institutions and programmes should be tied to funding. This approach has been demonstrated to influence institutional behaviour and shift their focus from enrolment to other outcomes considered desirable (such as completion, or labour market outcomes in the case of vocational programmes). Box 6.3 provides some examples of how education institutions in OECD countries have used outcome-based funding.

It should be noted that there are risks in outcome-based funding. If the outcome measures are graduation rates, this has to be combined with strong quality assurance mechanisms, to ensure that institutions do not artificially make programmes easier or alter their intake policies, to improve graduation rates. Another risk is that in regions that face many challenges, institutions end up being underfunded because outcomes are generally poorer. To avoid this risk, a diversified set of outcome-based measures should be used, including indicators related to the characteristics of students (e.g. the share of disadvantaged students).

Recommended steps

Table 6.2 provides some possible action steps that could be taken to develop and implement a quality assurance system in CET. For each action step, the most relevant stakeholders concerned are listed. The list of stakeholders is not exhaustive, and cooperation between different stakeholders is encouraged. The actions steps focus on the short- and medium-term, and a more ambitious action plan could be developed for the longer term in line with the vision for CET from the DHET's strategic documents.

Box 6.3. Performance-based funding of education and training providers

United States

Since 2015, approximately 37 states have adopted some version of performance-based funding of their two- or four-year colleges. The majority of states allocate 5% to 10% of total state support based on performance. Most of the performance measures used by states are related to completion, progression and labour market outcomes. The latter is usually measured by looking at employment rates and wages of graduates. Some states give more weight in their performance measures to specific groups of disadvantaged students, such as low-income students, and to certain in-demand skills (e.g. STEM qualifications). Evaluations of the performance-based funding model have highlighted the importance of effective policy design when introducing performance-based objectives, as they may not always have the intended effects. It is found, for example, that the performance-based measures in the United States have led to a shift towards short-term certificates (which have relatively low labour market value), as this might be the easiest way for colleges to secure funding.

Finland

Up until 2017, performance-based funding in Finnish vocational further education and training was limited to 3% of public funding allocated to the VET providers. The rest of the government-funded budget was based on student numbers and unit prices. A major VET reform that was approved in 2017 plans to increase the importance of performance-based funding significantly over the period 2018-22. By 2022, 50% of the public budget will be performance- or efficiency-based. Performance-based funding (35%) will be based on how many qualifications are delivered, and efficiency-based funding (15%) will take into account access to employment and further education and training.

Korea

Junior colleges in Korea are post-secondary vocational education institutions that mainly offer two-year programmes. The majority of junior colleges are private, and some of them receive government funding. The government provides two types of funding: grants to "Colleges of Excellence" and formula funding. The formula for the latter type of funding was recently revised and is now based on nine indicators covering a wide range of areas: performance of education (19%), student support (17%), education conditions (15%), curriculum (12%), management of lecturers and students' assessment (10%), integrity of the college (10%), cooperation between the college and industry (8%), college development plans (6%), and contribution in the local community (3%). Each indicator is measured through multiple sub-indicators. The outcome of education, for example, is measured by the employment rate of graduates, the ratio of the number of enrolments and the number of places (as set by quota), and satisfaction with the educational programmes.

Source: National Conference of State Legislation (2015[33]); OECD (2017[34]); Li and Kennedy (2018[35]); Ministry of Education and Culture (2017[36]); Kis and Park (2012[37]).

Table 6.2. Action steps for building a quality assurance framework

Action steps and relevant stakeholders

Action steps	Main stakeholders
Map out existing quality assurance and accreditation processes and improve their transparency (including the registration of skills programmes by SETAs).	DHET, SAQA, Quality Councils
Clarify the sharing of responsibilities between the different Quality Councils (and the SETAs) when it comes to the programmes under CET, to improve clarify and reduce transaction costs.	DHET, SAQA, Quality Councils, SETAs
Develop, in consultation with stakeholders, quality standards and self-evaluation tools for CET institutions to measure performance against these standards. This can be part of the process of defining a clear mandate and shape for the CET sector.	DHET, CLCs, CET colleges, lecturers, unions and other stakeholders
Develop an accreditation system based on the quality standards, to ensure that all institutions are of quality and meet minimum requirements, and involve lecturers in self-evaluation.	DHET, quality assurance agencies
Ensure that all programmes meet some set quality standards that include targets, in terms of completion rates and labour market outcomes for vocational programmes.	DHET, quality assurance agencies
Assess the CET network in its entirety, to identify gaps and duplications, and look at mechanisms to adapt future provision to the local needs taking into account the existing programmes (see Chapter 5).	DHET, CET colleges, CLCs
Develop a monitoring system for institutions to help them improve and collect data about learners, lecturers and institutions, including on learners' socio-economic background.	DHET, CET colleges, CLCs

Note: DHET: Department for Higher Education and Training; DBE: Department for Basic Education CLC: Community Learning Centre; SAQA: South African Qualifications Authority.

References

Buthelezi, Z. (2018), "Lecturer experiences of TVET College challenges in the post-apartheid era: a case of unintended consequences of educational reform in South Africa", *Journal of Vocational Education & Training*, pp. 1-20, http://dx.doi.org/10.1080/13636820.2018.1437062. [16]

Cort, P., A. Härkönen and K. Volmari (2004), *PROFF – Professionalization of VET Teachers for the Future*. [15]

Council for Higher Education Accreditation (2010), *The Value of Accreditation*, Washington DC, http://www.chea.org/pdf/Value%20of%20US%20Accreditation%2006.29.2010_buttons.pdf. [28]

Department of Higher Education and Training (2017), "National Improvement Plan For Teaching and Learning for CET", http://www.dhet.gov.za/SiteAssets/Community%20College/National-Improvement-Plan-For-Teaching-and-Learning-for-CET.pdf. [31]

Department of Higher Education and Training (2016), "National Policy for the Monitoring and Evaluation of CET colleges", http://www.dhet.gov.za/SiteAssets/Community%20College/National%20Policy%20for%20the%20Monitoring%20and%20Evaluation%20%20of%20CET%20Colleges.pdf. [32]

Department of Higher Education and Training (2016), *National Policy for the Monitoring and Evaluation of CET Colleges*. [22]

Department of Higher Education and Training (2015), *National Policy on Community Colleges*, http://www.dhet.gov.za/Community/national%20policy%20on%20community%20colleges.pdf. [9]

Department of Higher Education and Training (2015), "Policy on Minimum Requirements for Programmes Leading to Qualifications for Educators and Lecturers in Adult and Community Education and Training", http://www.dhet.gov.za/Teacher%20Education/Policy%20on%20minimum%20requirements%20for%20programmes%20leading%20to%20qualification.pdf. [8]

Department of Higher Education and Training (2013), *White Paper for Post-School Education and Training*. [6]

Department of Higher Education and Training (2012), *Green Paper for Post-School Education and Training*. [14]

DHET (2019), *TVET Lecturer Development*, http://www.dhet.gov.za/TVET%20Conference/Commission%204/Alice%20Msibi-KZN%20TVET%20Lecturer%20Development.pdf. [18]

DHET (2018), *Lecturer and Moderator Training*, http://www.tvetcolleges.co.za/Uploads/ExamTimetable/Home/15/172/ICASS%20Facilitator%20Guide%20FINAL.pdf. [19]

Eichhorst, W. et al. (2012), "A roadmap to vocational education and training around the world", *IZA Discussion Paper, No. 7110. IZA, Bonn*, http://ftp.iza.org/dp7110.pdf. [27]

Field, S., P. Musset and J. Álvarez-Galván (2014), *A Skills beyond School Review of South Africa*, OECD Reviews of Vocational Education and Training, OECD Publishing, Paris, http://dx.doi.org/10.1787/9789264223776-en. [17]

JEED (2018), *2018 Outline of Services*, Japan Organization for Employment of the Elderly, Persons with Disabilities and Job Seekers, https://www.jeed.or.jp/english/u603g2000000008u-att/u603g200000000fi.pdf (accessed on 30 October 2018). [30]

Kis, V. and E. Park (2012), *A Skills beyond School Review of Korea*, OECD Reviews of Vocational Education and Training , Paris, http://www.oecd.org/education/skills-beyond-school/SBS%20Korea.pdf (accessed on 23 July 2018). [37]

Li, A. and A. Kennedy (2018), "Performance Funding Policy Effects on Community College Outcomes: Are Short-Term Certificates on the Rise?", *Community College Review*, Vol. 46/1, pp. 3-39, http://dx.doi.org/10.1177/0091552117743790. [35]

Lugg, R. (2009), *Making different equal? Fractured state and ruptured policy: The National Qualifications Framework in South Africa*, pp. 260–267. [25]

McCarthy, M. and P. Musset (2016), *A Skills beyond School Review of Peru*, OECD Reviews of Vocational Education and Training, OECD Publishing, Paris, http://dx.doi.org/10.1787/9789264265400-en. [29]

Ministry of Education and Culture (2017), *What in vocational education and training will change for education providers*, https://minedu.fi/documents/1410845/4297550/OKM_AKR_what+will+change+for+education+providers.pdf/c2419142-26b2-483c-975b-e1624d81c5ee/OKM_AKR_what+will+change+for+education+providers.pdf.pdf (accessed on 9 July 2018). [36]

Musset, P. (2010), "Initial Teacher Education and Continuing Training Policies in a Comparative Perspective: Current Practices in OECD Countries and a Literature Review on Potential Effects", *OECD Education Working Papers*, No. 48, OECD Publishing, Paris, http://dx.doi.org/10.1787/5kmbphh7s47h-en. [10]

National Conference of State Legislation (2015), *Performance-Based Funding for Higher Education*, http://www.ncsl.org/research/education/performance-funding.aspx (accessed on 9 July 2018). [33]

OECD (2019), *Getting Skills Right: Future-Ready Adult Learning Systems*, Getting Skills Right, OECD Publishing, Paris, https://dx.doi.org/10.1787/9789264311756-en. [3]

OECD (2017), *Financial Incentives for Steering Education and Training*, Getting Skills Right, OECD Publishing, Paris, http://dx.doi.org/10.1787/9789264272415-en. [34]

OECD (2014), *Skills beyond School: Synthesis Report*, OECD Reviews of Vocational Education and Training, OECD Publishing, Paris, http://dx.doi.org/10.1787/9789264214682-en. [1]

OECD (2013), *Synergies for Better Learning: An International Perspective on Evaluation and Assessment*, OECD Reviews of Evaluation and Assessment in Education, OECD Publishing, Paris, http://dx.doi.org/10.1787/9789264190658-en. [2]

OECD (2010), *Improving Schools: Strategies for Action in Mexico*, OECD Publishing, Paris, http://dx.doi.org/10.1787/9789264087040-en. [24]

OECD (2010), *Learning for Jobs*, OECD Reviews of Vocational Education and Training, OECD Publishing, Paris, http://dx.doi.org/10.1787/9789264087460-en. [13]

OECD (2005), *Teachers Matter: Attracting, Developing and Retaining Effective Teachers*, Education and Training Policy, OECD Publishing, Paris, http://dx.doi.org/10.1787/9789264018044-en. [4]

Parliamentary Monitoring Group (2018), "Community Education and Training (CET) latest developments: Department briefing", http://Community Education and Training (CET) latest developments: Department briefing. [5]

Parliamentary Monitoring Group (2017), *Community Education and Training (CET) update by Department of Higher Education and Training*, https://pmg.org.za/committee-meeting/25628/. [7]

Pont, B., D. Nusche and H. Moorman (2008), *Improving School Leadership*, OECD Publishing. [23]

Republic of South Africa (2000), "Criteria for the Recognition and Evaluation of Qualifications for Employment in Education based on the Norms and Standards for Educators", *Government Gazette*, No. 21565, https://www.gov.za/sites/default/files/gcis_document/201409/215650.pdf (accessed on 8 January 2019). [11]

SACE (2019), *SACE CPTD*, https://www.getsacepoints.co.za/sace-cptd/. [12]

South Carolina Department of Education (2018), *South Carolina Career and Technology Education Work-Based Certification Pre-Service / In-Service Training Program.* [21]

Tara Fenwick, E. (ed.) (2014), *Governing Knowledge: Comparison, knowledge-based technologies and expertise in the regulation of education*, Routledge, Oxford. [26]

Xu, Z., J. Hannaway and C. Taylor (2007), "Making a Difference? The Effects of Teach for America in High School", *National Center for Analysis of Longitudinal Data in Education Research.* [20]

Annex A. Recent CET (draft) legislation

This annex provides a summary of (draft) legislation published in recent years on the topic of CET.

Curricula

- *National policy on curriculum development and implementation in CET colleges* (May 2017)*:* The objective of CET programmes is to improve livelihoods, promote labour market inclusion and support community and individual needs. The colleges will therefore provide programmes in four areas: i) literacy and post-literacy programmes, ii) academic qualifications (at the high school level), iii) occupational and skills programmes, and iv) non-formal programmes. In addition, CET colleges may evolve to provide higher education qualifications. In order to implement the diverse curricula effectively, the colleges should appoint suitable subject specialists and develop teaching and learning plans.

Staffing and quality of teaching and learning

- *Draft Policy on Staffing Norms for Community Education and Training Colleges* (March 2016)*:* The budget for compensation of employees will be capped at 75% of the total CET budget. 80% of this budget is reserved for lecturing staff and 20% for support staff. Post allocations to CLCs are done based on "weighted students", taking into account that some students and learning programmes require more favourable post allocations than others. Norms are set for minimum and maximum class sizes (depending on the type of programme), and guidelines are provided in terms of operating hours, providing for part-time and weekend operations.
- *Policy on minimum requirements for programmes leading to qualifications for educators and lecturers in adult and CET* (March 2015): A set of entry-level qualifications, initial professional teaching qualifications, post-professional qualifications and postgraduate degrees are introduced and will replace all qualifications formerly recognised and approved for teaching in AET and in CET. Progression pathways between the different qualifications is clearly set out, and work-integrated learning forms an important components of the qualifications. Acknowledging that many students who enrol for AET/CET qualifications will have relevant work experience and/or studied related subjects, opportunities for RPL and credit accumulation and transfer are made available.
- *National Improvement Plan for Teaching and Learning for CET Colleges* (January 2017): Formal qualifications will be the starting point of the CET institutions, and the institutions should decide on the streams they wish to offer. The institutions should gradually expand to also offer non-formal programmes that respond to the needs of the community and labour market. Advocacy plans

should be put in place to inform and attract potential students. The quality of curriculum delivery will be monitored by the CET college management. New qualified lecturers should be attracted to the system, and the lecturers that are already in the system should participate in training activities. Adequate allocation should be set aside for procurement of learning and teaching support material. The performance of teachers, learners and centres should be monitored and evaluated rigorously.

Administration and student support

- *Draft policy framework for the development of admission policies by CET colleges* (March 2017): The College Council determines the admission requirements to the College, in line with the DHET's policies and regulations. A students' attendance and punctuality policy should be put in place to monitor attendance after admission. A registry should be kept that records all admitted and registered students.
- *Draft national policy on student support services for CET colleges* (June 2017): Student support services should be put in place to help students make informed choices. The support services consist of pre-entry support, on-course support, exit support, community support and career guidance. The pre-entry support services consist of profiling the students and administering placement tests. The results from the placement test can be used to re-orientate a student towards are more suitable education and training level. During their time as students at CET colleges, students should receive academic and personal development support, as well as support and preparation for examinations. It is of crucial importance for students to have access to learning and teaching support materials. Upon completion of the CET programme, students should receive information about further education and training opportunities, including entrepreneurial skills programmes, as well as job opportunities. In addition, student tracking systems should be introduced. Student support services should become a core function of the CET system, and appropriate funding and staff resources should be guaranteed.

Infrastructure

- *The draft policy and procedures for regulating the opening, merging and closing of CET colleges and learning sites* (March 2017): The Minister may merge or close CET colleges, but the decision to open, merge or close CET learning sites lies with the College Council. To open a new learning site, College Councils need to provide empirical evidence that justifies the opening, including evidence on proper infrastructure, sufficient resources, the identification of responsive education and training programmes, and support from the communities. Similarly, the merging and closing of learning sites should be based on empirical evidence, and the communities, staff and students should be warned in due course.

Monitoring and evaluation

- *The national policy for monitoring and evaluation of CET colleges* (October 2016): The CET system will be monitored and evaluated using a range of data collection tools, including surveys, annual and quarterly reports, audits and information systems. Monitoring and evaluation will happen in three key areas: i) education, training and development, ii) planning, institutional development and support, and iii) financial management capacity and systems. Detailed areas include students' performance, strategic partnerships and linkages, advocacy and community mobilisation, and the functionality of the council.

- *Draft national policy on the verification of enrolments and staff in the CET colleges* (February 2017): A verification system needs to be established to ensure the authenticity of enrolled students and staff of CET institutions. The CLCs should keep detailed information on students, such as their enrolment forms, admission register and class lists, and staff members. Students and staff must complete a verification form once a year, which will be used to verify the authenticity of admission and enrolment data. In addition, the DHET will verify a random selection of students.
- *Draft national policy on annual reporting and submission of annual performance reports by CET colleges* (September 2017): CET colleges must prepare a strategic plan that lays out its mission, vision, priorities and project plans for at least a five-year period. Annual performance plans must be prepared that cover planning and budgeting aligned with the strategic plan. These annual plans must contain performance indicators and targets. Every year, a report needs to be submitted that assesses the performance of the colleges.

ORGANISATION FOR ECONOMIC CO-OPERATION AND DEVELOPMENT

The OECD is a unique forum where governments work together to address the economic, social and environmental challenges of globalisation. The OECD is also at the forefront of efforts to understand and to help governments respond to new developments and concerns, such as corporate governance, the information economy and the challenges of an ageing population. The Organisation provides a setting where governments can compare policy experiences, seek answers to common problems, identify good practice and work to co-ordinate domestic and international policies.

The OECD member countries are: Australia, Austria, Belgium, Canada, Chile, the Czech Republic, Denmark, Estonia, Finland, France, Germany, Greece, Hungary, Iceland, Ireland, Israel, Italy, Japan, Korea, Latvia, Lithuania, Luxembourg, Mexico, the Netherlands, New Zealand, Norway, Poland, Portugal, the Slovak Republic, Slovenia, Spain, Sweden, Switzerland, Turkey, the United Kingdom and the United States. The European Union takes part in the work of the OECD.

OECD Publishing disseminates widely the results of the Organisation's statistics gathering and research on economic, social and environmental issues, as well as the conventions, guidelines and standards agreed by its members.

OECD PUBLISHING, 2, rue André-Pascal, 75775 PARIS CEDEX 16
(81 2019 06 1 P) ISBN 978-92-64-31229-6 – 2019

www.ingramcontent.com/pod-product-compliance
Ingram Content Group UK Ltd.
Pitfield, Milton Keynes, MK11 3LW, UK
UKHW051240300926
15471UKWH00015B/1446

9 789264 312296